M  N

Donald Reeves was born in May 1934 and educated at Sherborne School. He served in the Royal Sussex Regiment (1952–4) and then studied at Queens' College, Cambridge. He was a British Council lecturer in Beirut (1957–60), and tutor at Brasted Theological College (1960–1). After training at Cuddesdon Theological College he was ordained in 1963. He has since served churches in Maidstone (1963–5) and Morden (1965–80), and was Chaplain to the Bishop of Southwark (1965–8).

Since 1980 Donald Reeves has been Rector of St James's Church, Piccadilly, where he carries out a unique ministry, both to the many people who work locally and to the thousands of visitors who come to London every year. He is the author of *For God's Sake* (1988).

D1367990

MAKING SENSE OF RELIGION

OF RELIGION

A Fresh Look at Christianity

Donald Reeves

BBC BOOKS

ACKNOWLEDGEMENTS

I would like to acknowledge publicly those who have encouraged me in the writing of this book: Peter Pelz, whose creativity and humanity have been a constant inspiration, and Nadir Dinshaw, whose friendship has been invaluable. Many friends at St James's Church, Piccadilly, have suffered my period of absence with a healthy mixture of resignation, good humour and encouragement.

I am most grateful to my secretary, Linda Maude, who has worked well beyond the call of duty to prepare the manuscript. However, the book would never have been completed but for Tracy Redfearn, whose research and editing skills, clarity and care have been indispensable. I would also like to thank BBC Books, especially Martha Caute and Kelly Davis for all their editorial work. Any inconsistencies, infelicities of style and unintended confusions are mine and mine alone.

Donald Reeves

Front cover illustration by Paul Bateman

Published by BBC Books,
a division of BBC Enterprises Limited
Woodlands, 80 Wood Lane, London W12 0TT

First published 1989

Reprinted 1989

© Donald Reeves 1989

ISBN 0 563 20759 0

Set in 11 on 13pt Janson by Ace Filmsetting Ltd, Frome, Somerset
Cover printed by Fletchers Ltd, Norwich, Norfolk
Printed and bound in Great Britain by Redwood Burn Ltd,
Trowbridge, Wiltshire

CONTENTS

1 MAKING

SENSE

This book takes a fresh look at Christianity. It tentatively explores new ways in which it may be possible to speak of God. But it also attempts to show how necessary it is for Christianity to become fully conscious of its inheritance, so that ancient memories can be reclaimed. It considers in what sense Jesus Christ is central to Christianity in the light of many difficult and unanswered questions about him.

While writing this book I have tried to retain an awareness of the unprecedented scale of suffering in the world, and the evil which has caused much of it. I know that suffering and evil have always been obstacles to faith; I have suggested an approach which does not flinch from them. I have also tried to define some characteristics of holiness, and though this book is not specifically about the Church it draws attention to the need to recover the true meaning of celebration.

I have written this book out of a conviction, shared by many, that the world is in the midst of rapid change, the outcome of which is very uncertain. This awareness springs from two different but related issues: what we have done and are doing to the Earth, for Mother Earth is dying; and what we have done and are doing to the poor of the world – not only the poor in London and in the north of England, but in all the world's major cities and in the Third World. Many other people, while not having the same conviction about these changes, may still feel a deep sense of confusion and concern about the state of the world – that there is a profound anomaly in their lives.

There are those who deny that we live in critical times. For them it is 'business as usual', and since they have benefited substantially from systems which have helped to create the world's difficulties, they will do everything in their power to prevent criticism and change. To recognise this anomaly requires generosity, courage and sacrifice; it means letting go of much that has been taken for granted in the way that we have arranged our affairs – in politics and economics, for example, as well as the assumptions behind them.

My concern is more limited. It is to explore the part that Christianity could play in a changing world, and in any possible renaissance of society. I am very aware of the presence of other ancient religious traditions both in England and elsewhere. A broad ecumenical approach is called for, whereby Jews, Buddhists, Muslims, Hindus, the followers of tribal religions, as well as Christians, could learn from one another and together become a power for good. But 'interfaith dialogue' is still in its infancy. We are not yet ready to proceed in this direction.

So, for the present, my concern is with Christianity. I believe that its experience and practice can preserve our capacity to remain human, so that a future is created where all humanity and all Creation can co-exist in harmony. I realise how idealistic such sentiments may sound. I have expressed them directly and simply because I believe Christianity makes sense of the universe and of our experience – of how things hold together.

To make sense of the whole of human experience (encompassing both good and evil) is a huge undertaking but nevertheless this has always been the aim of religion and the reason for its persistence in so many different forms. Part of the fascination of religion is that it offers formulas for human fulfilment and happiness. These formulas are often set up as absolute rules which must be followed and obeyed to get benefits and rewards; and they can rapidly assume the status of a fixed, unalterable system in which humanity is easily lost.

However, more precise obstacles to Christianity are sometimes expressed by those who are largely indifferent to it, or by those who only meet it occasionally. There is, for example, the charge that Christianity is obscurantist, and fuels fatalism and superstition. There is also the accusation of irrelevance: the way Christian beliefs and formulas are expressed belong to another age, and bear no relation to the problems and opportunities of the world today. In addition, Christianity is accused of excluding people, women in particular. There is the familiar critique of the Church as an obstacle to belief in God. David Jenkins, the Bishop of Durham, expresses this trenchantly in *God, Politics and the Future*:

> Anyone who, like myself, continues to be compelled to believe in God, to seek God and to respond to God, must surely be deeply troubled by the endemic ungodliness and inhumanity of so much of organised religion . . . churches . . . whether at the level of their organised hierarchies, synods and committees, or at the local level of their congregations, seem to be largely occupied with their own maintenance, manipulation and needs. Churches therefore tend to look like institutions preoccupied with providing packages of spiritual comfort for the private consumption of their active adherents while indulging in defensive battles against those realities of the world which seem to threaten their faith, combined with intensive battles among themselves about what anyone but themselves would consider to be either secondary or even pseudo-problems.[1]

There are those who say that Christian belief is a neurosis, a drug, that churches are mechanisms for keeping the poor in their place (a regular reading of the *Daily Telegraph* would certainly confirm this observation) and that the chief function of Christianity (together with the Royal Family, the BBC, and the House of Lords) is to provide social cohesion. There are also those of a more philosophical bent who say that religion has never recovered from the battering it received as a result of the new thinking of the Enlightenment.

Finally there are those who interpret the practice of religion as essentially anti-life and anti-fulfilment. It seems to thrive on rigidities and dogmatism which cause wars and persecution. It spawns hypocrisy – religious people who profess the unity of the human race yet tolerate the killing of one another. There is ignorance, rigidity and fatalism. Religious arrogance is particularly apparent in regard to the multi-faith society.

If Christianity is to make any sense today, it has to unmask those idols which surround us, and have become part of us. It has to confront its beliefs and practices with the discoveries of the natural sciences and biblical and literary criticism. Truth cannot be stopped. Christianity has to be expressed with persuasive power so that faith in God leads to vitality, and is seen to be on the side of life, and its fulfilment. This means giving attention to the new sensibilities of our age – appreciating the planet on which we depend and taking responsibility for its future.

It is not possible to be absolutely secure and certain about religious convictions and belief. That is not to say that it is irrational to be a 'believer': there are intelligent reasons for being religious, and I hope some of them will become clear in this book. There is, however, no final proof that God exists. Fundamentalist believers of any religion who insist otherwise are mistaken. Those Christians who say the Bible is an absolute truth, the literal Word of God, incontrovertible and different from all other texts, have turned the Bible into an idol, and their own religion into a monstrous creation which may serve to protect them, but at what a cost to the freedom of the tough, yet fragile, human spirit.

When I am faced with the question 'Does God exist?' the most I can do is agree with the last paragraph of Ruben Alves' *What Is Religion?*, which ponders these questions:

> Does God exist? Does life have meaning? Does the universe have a face? Is death my sister? To which the religious soul can only reply, 'I do not know. But I ardently desire that this be true. And I make the leap unreservedly. For it is more beautiful to risk on the side of hope than to have certainty on the side of a cold, senseless universe.'[2]

No absolute claims about truth and meaning are made.

Instead, we are offered the choices by which we can give meaning to our lives; interpreting the universe as either cold and senseless or full of personal value and human hope.

Language and thought are so often inadequate to express experiential reality. They can only point towards such hopeful meaning and then often obscure it. We can use language to say what we believe we experience, but we do not know what the nature of that experience is. Simone Weil writes of this difficulty with great immediacy:

> There is a God. There is no God. What is the problem? I am quite sure that there is a God in the sense that I am sure my love is no illusion. I am quite sure there is no God in the sense that I am sure there is nothing that resembles what I can conceive when I say that word.[3]

In other words, while she is sure her belief is not an illusion she is equally certain that none of her conceptions, pictures, images or words describing God resemble God. At best they may offer hints and clues. Sallie McFague, in a note to Chapter 1 of her *Models of God*, expresses this slightly differently:

> God is and remains a mystery. We really do not know: the hints and clues we have of the way things are – whether we call them experiences, revelation, or whatever – are too fragile, too little (and more often than not, too negative) for much more than a hypothesis, a guess, a projection of a possibility that, although it can be comprehensive and illuminating, may not be true. We can believe it is and act as if it were, but it is, to use Ricoeur's term, a 'wager'.[4]

Faith, then, is not an absolute certainty, a fact that can be described and defined, but a wager, an option or choice which is taken hopefully but which nevertheless contains within itself elements of uncertainty and doubt.

The Bishop of Durham reminds his readers of this strain of agnosticism in all religious belief. When quoting from Professor Hodges he says:

> It is agreed doctrine that God is beyond human understanding. This is not merely the hasty reaction of the ordinary man, disheartened at the sight of the problems which arise. It is also the considered judgement of the philosophical theologians who, on the

grounds of metaphysics and theory of knowledge, work out the
doctrine of Divine Incomprehensibility.[5]

With such an alliance between desire for certainty about God
and an awareness of the inadequacy of language, doubt
becomes an integral part of religious life. Kenneth Leech
writes:

> True faith can only grow and mature if it includes the elements of
> paradox and creative doubt. Hence the insistence of orthodoxy
> that God cannot be known by the mind, but is known in the obscu-
> rity of faith, in the way of ignorance, in the darkness. Such doubt is
> not the enemy of faith but an essential element within it. For faith
> in God does not bring false peace of answered questions . . . Rather
> it can be seen as a process of unceasing interrogation . . . Without
> creative doubt religion becomes hard and cruel, degenerating into
> the spurious security which breeds intolerance and persecution.[6]

Leech makes the point that doubt is essential to faith and religion. It is doubt that keeps religion a dynamic, creative process
that does not crystallise into a hard fanatical system of absolute
values.

However, we live in a time of cultural barbarism where 'facts'
and simple certainties are what count. Questioning, probing,
bringing out into the open the elusive nature of religious belief,
is regarded as destabilising and subversive, even anarchic. But
to those who perceive faith in the way I am beginning to indicate, this approach draws on an ancient tradition. It is a
tradition that speaks in symbols, such as the journey. Monica
Furlong's *Travelling In* puts it like this:

> The religious man is the one who believes that life is about making
> some kind of journey; the non-religious man is the one who
> believes there is no journey to take.

> What all the accounts [of the inward journey] have in common is a
> sense of the terrors to be encountered *en route*. There is the terror of
> darkness and loss . . . the terror of infatuation . . . in which progress
> is halted as we lose ourselves among our projections . . . the terror
> of foul and unsuspected monsters to be grappled with . . . . Then
> there is a kind of passive terror – the terror of accepting mortality,
> weakness, old age.

The journey is an ancient picture of the essence of the religious life, encapsulating all human experience and emotions. The resonance of this symbol partly accounts for the popularity of pilgrimages in the Middle Ages. Gerard Hughes, in his account of his own walk to Rome, writes:

> Walking on foot to some 'holy' place answers a deep religious need. The Greeks went to Delphi, Muslims go to Mecca, some English people go to Stonehenge. It is a symbolic gesture, a search for our real destination, a kind of sacramental journey, a sign that we are in search of an answer to our deepest longings, and the journey is undertaken in the belief that there is an Answer. On the road the pilgrims learn that searching for God is already to have found him and that direction is much more important than destination, because God is not just an end, not a beginning, but for us he is always beginning without end.[8]

Furthermore, the symbol of the journey invites a decision as to whether or not life has meaning. In *Jesus – The Unanswered Questions*, John Bowden writes:

> In a famous modern parable John Hick [the theologian] illustrated the contrast between these perspectives by describing two travellers on the same road, the only road there is. One believes that it leads to the Celestial City, interpreting the pleasant parts as encouragements and the obstacles as trials of his purpose and lessons in endurance, bringing about a process of growth: the other finds only the road itself and the luck of the road in good weather and bad. We all have to identify with one or other of these travellers if we are to follow the questioning where it leads or decide that it is not worth bothering with; to decide whether we see the world as having meaning or being meaningless . . . No one who has not at some time or other truly struggled with the prospect, the threat, of meaninglessness, can be aware of the risk of the venture of faith.[9]

However, the analogy of belief as a journey is not so accessible, not so obvious as it might seem, in spite of its archetypal associations, not least because we have lost the capacity to reflect on and absorb our own experience. One of the greatest benefits of any sort of counselling is the opportunity to return to the past, to heal bad memories, to grow into some awareness and acceptance of yourself, and thus to see how change and growth have occurred.

But this understanding of experience as a journey is not available for many – perhaps only for those who have the time and money to engage in counselling of one sort or another. For many, keeping on and on, and just surviving, is about as much as can be expected. I remember an elderly widow who had recently been bereaved. We sat in her front room and she talked about her husband and then herself. She spoke of their life together, their children and her grandchildren. Then, suddenly looking away from me, out of the window, she cried with frustration and anger, 'Oh, I don't know – it has been such a waste.' Her family had always been poor, struggling to make ends meet. She had never had the chance to tell her story, or to see that her own experience was unique and precious. She had no self-regard, little sense of her own courage and resilience. She had borne her suffering in silence. This silence resulted from her own powerlessness and her inability to change her situation.

Graham Greene, in *The Honorary Consul*, contrasts those who lack speech with the articulate middle classes:

> Most of the middle-class patients were accustomed to spending ten minutes explaining a simple attack of flu. It was only in the 'barrio' of the poor, that we ever encountered suffering in silence, suffering which had no vocabulary to explain a degree of pain, its position or its nature.[10]

The widow I visited would not have understood what it meant to say that her life was a journey moving towards some remote but uncertain destination. (She had no way of relating this idea to reality.) Like many others, she had experienced the traditional rites of passage: baptism, marriage, and funerals; but in a trivial, perfunctory way. To her children, the progress from adolescence to adulthood was now marked by joining the ranks of first-time buyers and becoming the proud owners of a mortgage. So religion, as well as offering fundamental positive images, also negatively confirms the fatalism, powerlessness and apathy which undermine and destroy hope.

Albert Nolan, in *God in South Africa*, writes:

> The temptation or tendency to preach a timeless gospel is the same as the tendency . . . to say something that is equally applicable to everybody. . . . Western theology seems to be based upon the assumption that nothing is true or valuable unless it applies to all people, at all times and in all circumstances. What one ends up with is an abstract God who deals with abstract 'man' in an abstract world.[11]

This universalising tendency of much of Western Christianity diminishes memory and discourages reflection. It prevents those who are living without dignity and without hope from recognising that their experience of suffering and injustice is the first step forward on their journey. Thus, the reclaiming of our particular memories, both individual and collective, is a priority for making sense of our experience and Christianity.

How, then, can we recover, and understand, our experience and memory? Desire or longing – this represents the point of embarkation on the religious journey. The longing is for communion and union. The very basis of religion is the longing to experience the order and harmony, the grace which is built into the Creation. It is a longing for unity – to heal the divisions in ourselves, to establish justice and then peace between one another, to treat the planet with care and respect, to be one with all Creation. That is how I would begin to describe the longing that humankind has for God.

As I have experienced it, this longing is often expressed in terms of vocation. How can I do good? How can I work effectively here or there for peace or for justice? What shall I do? What is the best way for me, now, to respond to that prompting, that 'call', as it is usually described? When these questions have been shared with me, the questioner, often with minimal experience of Christianity, uses religious language. The longing to contribute to anything that makes for more beauty, grace or love, is more than just fitful idealism. It is an impulse of the human spirit to transcend selfish concerns and preconceptions, to move towards our neighbours – these days nothing less than the planet!

I believe this longing is invariably described in religious

terms because other explanations do not do it justice; they reduce it. The longing is utopian and idealistic. It is about the goal and purpose of our existence, and wherever this longing is deeply felt Christianity begins to look as though it could make sense.

I have described some of the obstacles to Christian belief, and tried to show that doubt, insecurity and uncertainty are essential to faith in God; of necessity our expressions of faith are always inadequate. Some readers may be impatient for slick answers, quick solutions and clever tricks to make Christianity more palatable. I cannot provide them, for religious language, and the truth it conveys, are not of that order.

The symbol of the journey has been proposed as a way to interpret and understand our lives, but this is accessible only to those who have had the opportunity to absorb and reflect on their experience. Thus, it is necessary to find ways in which particular individual and collective memories can be reclaimed. As 'stories' are told, and suffering finds a voice, so hope may be born. And, for me, the key to the journey is the desire and longing for communion and union with Creation, one another and with God.

But today the Church is not an institution which works away at articulating and helping to put into some sort of practice what it means to seek communion and union. English Christianity has in general become a tame, puny thing, obsessed with its own identity, power struggles and survival. The grandeur and simplicity of its affirmations and promises have been muffled and lost. The next chapter considers why religion has become so domesticated, and what can be done to recover its wildness, its beauty and its truth.

2 | IDOLATRY AND IMAGINATION

The chief factor which accounts for the way Christianity has become trivialised, and which prevents it from being the coherent and vital faith it could be, is the idolatry of money. One of the most sustained, rigorous and eloquent discussions of this idolatry is to be found in Jeremy Seabrook's and Trevor Blackwell's *The Politics of Hope*. In this book they explore the relationship between capitalism and religion:

> The decay of the more traditional forms of the spiritual life seems to have released people's energies and feelings to seek equivalent satisfactions in other areas of human activity. In our period, capitalism has found in this free-floating religiosity, which is characterised above all by desires for transcendence and communion, new marketing opportunities.[1]

Capitalism has ingested the symbols of people's feelings, thoughts and inspirations. It has come to function not as the antagonist or ally but as the incarnation of religion. The expectations of capitalism – for example, for a higher and higher standard of living – appear to form the very substance of life, as reflected in the structures of society. And people begin to believe that grace and beatitude are only possible through the pursuit of wealth.

Religious language is used to convey the dominance of money and the marketplace in our culture. The myth of capital informs our whole lives, but of course we do not perceive it as such. Money has become the one sacrament whereby access is gained to the beatific vision of capitalism. Money becomes the release from the ordinariness of living. The rich are blessed for they are inheriting the Earth, and money is the grace by which this blessing is mediated. Buy the right things, experiences and sensations and we shall transcend this mundane humanity and know what it is to be happy. This message is to be found in the iconography of the advertising industry.

Jeremy Seabrook's description of the Victoria Shopping Centre in Nottingham illustrates the way capitalism has built its own shrines – temples of the marketplace which embody and celebrate grace, transcendence and promises of eternity:

> What is most striking is the silence of the crowds. You can hear a mildly euphoric music above the shuffling feet on the marble causeways, and the splashing of a great coloured cascade in the middle of the ground floor. The space is like the nave of a cathedral; the shop fronts are stained-glass windows, full of stylised models in expressionist poses.

> The place is a permanent exhibition, part *kermis* [religious carnival], part communion. Here, all human pleasures and aspirations have been captured and priced. The display combines the search for happiness with a sense of the great public rituals that have decayed. The names of products – Jupiter, Saturn, Aztec, Odyssey, Vivaldi, Windsor, Savannah, Olympic, Capri, Imperial – represent a cosmic ransacking of time and place, to describe beds, duvets, fashion valances, chairs, dining tables, digital clocks; piracy that creates an impression of effortless mobility and power. Revolutions and miracles are advertised in the preparation of dessert foods and the washing of underwear; and in this way, politics and religion are put in their place.

> These are full of promise, not only of well-being and comfort, but even of immortality. Siliconised polypropylene, 'no deterioration', 'there for ever'. You are invited to sleep on a white cloud filled with soft Dacron, serenity Latex foam, four-poster beds, a home solarium, interior log saunas, marble caskets for bathing, water massage in sealed cabinets like up-ended coffins. Leisure and escape are everywhere; relaxation and sleep. Everything is caressing and somniferous. This place proposes a world which manages to

combine the beatific vision with the occupational therapy work-shop; it is the kind of setting in which my grandmother might have hoped she would spend eternity.[2]

Certainly for some the 'standard of living' has improved dra-matically since 1945. However, this relentless drive towards material prosperity has been achieved at great cost – the crea-tion of an under-class and the exploitation of the Third World. The planet itself is almost completely exhausted by the way it has been manhandled.

We rarely protest about the inhumanities which this so-called progress has created, for fear that we might thereby lose the material comforts that most of us enjoy. Thus a state of anxiety is maintained through fear. This fear in turn creates apathy, passivity and indifference; which erupt from time to time in acts of meaningless violence. What I have been trying to describe is the way in which the worship is hidden and taken for granted within capitalism, the system which acts as the con-duit for this idolatry. Christianity must unmask these idols, for a society which is possessed by money, as ours is, becomes idolatrous.

How do idols come about? Bob Goudzwarrd, in *Idols of our Time*, traces the progress of the making of idols:

> First, people sever something from their immediate environment, refashion it and erect it on its own feet in a special place. Secondly, they ritually consecrate it and kneel before it, seeing it as a thing which has life in itself. Third, they bring sacrifices and look to the idol for advice and direction. In short, they worship it. Worship brings with it a decrease in their own power; now the god reveals how they should live and act. And fourth, they expect the god to repay their reverence, obedience and sacrifices with health, secu-rity, prosperity and happiness. They give the idol permission to demand and receive whatever it desires, even if it includes animal or human life, because they see the idol as their saviour, as the one who can make life whole and bring blessing.[3]

Attitudes to technology have also become idolatrous. Tech-nology is a product of our inventive minds; it is a neutral thing which has been allowed to develop its own life. But unrestricted technology begins to promise more luxury, more prosperity, more health, as well as solutions to every sort of national and international problem. Before long nothing can stand in the way of its constant and continuing development, whatever sacrifices have to be made en route. Central to this transformaton of technology into an idol is fear. Slowly, imperceptibly, the roles are reversed. In the beginning we were in charge but as the idol grows we become dependent on it, anxious that it may collapse and we with it. Gradually the idol imprints its image on the maker; we begin to identify ourselves with the image we have made.

Psalm 115: 5–8 puts it simply:

> They have mouths, but they speak not:
> Eyes have they, but they see not:
> They have ears, but they hear not:
> Noses have they, but they smell not:
> They have hands, but they handle not:
> Feet have they, but they walk not:
> Neither speak they through their throat.
> They that make them are like unto them;
> So is every one that trusteth in them.

This brief analysis may seem too far-fetched but it is not so. For idolatry arises when something is lacking, when the framework of society does not allow us to express our deepest longing to reflect and absorb our experience – to tell our story.

Ken Leech, quoting Alasdair MacIntyre in *True God*, puts it like this:

> Those for whom life is emotionally empty may be at first content with limited perspectives; but later they may become cynical and disillusioned; and later still they may be the prey of any passing evangelist of unreason who will promise a coherent view of the world and a coherent programme for changing it.[4]

Capitalism displaces religion so that the experience of society is channelled into its own self-perpetuating system. Capitalism becomes religiosity when its idols in their various forms, particularly money, have created a new spirituality. John

Kamanough, in an article on 'Spirituality and Culture', argues that 'Advanced industrialist capitalist societies form a culture whose covert spirituality has inverted the virtues in such a way that pride, arrogance, revenge, greed, luck, covetousness and the same self-righteous hatred have become moral aspirations.'[5]

Morality has been turned upside-down. He tells of a successful Catholic who says to a young man hoping to help the poor, 'The greatest tragedy that could happen to you would be to end up somewhere dishing out food in a soup kitchen – you have a great future, don't waste it.' Capitalist spirituality, at its most extreme, makes material comfort its highest priority, leaving individuals with no sense of their own worth or value.

It has to be said, however, that the majority of those who describe themselves as Christians do not show any greater awareness of the idolatry of money than any other group in society. Even so, the sustained criticism of the Conservative Party since 1979 which has been expressed by Church leaders, clergy and many Church organisations of all denominations unconsciously points to the underlying anguish at the way in which our religious energies have been drained away, and diverted to the worship of money.

But how do we change? It is one thing to write about unmasking idolatries; it is another thing to do it. Change does not come from being exhorted or told what to do. It will not happen by scolding people to change their attitudes. We only change when our hearts are touched, when we acknowledge that we are accomplices in the service of other gods. And it is impossible to take this step without imagination. Imagination is the key to the recovery of a Christianity which deals with our experience as something real and vital. Yet it is this quality which is often missing from Christianity today.

Dennis Nineham, in *The Myth of God Incarnate*, says that it is in imagination that contemporary Christianity is weakest:

> People find it hard to believe in God because they do not have any lively imaginative pictures of the way God and the world as they know it are related. What they need most is a story, a picture, a

myth that will capture their imagination while meshing in with the rest of their sensibility in the way that messianic terms linked with the sensitivity of the first-century Jews, or Nicene symbolism with the sensibility of philosophically-minded fourth-century Greeks.[6]

Imagination is usually considered to be a frivolous quality associated with day-dreaming or fantasy. Ruben Alves writes: 'To affirm that someone's testimony is the product of the imagination and of fantasy is to accuse that person of mental problems or to suspect his or her moral integrity.'[7]

Whenever the imagination is called on to perform, the tone of the conversation or debate immediately relaxes, and everything is trivialised. I have experienced this publicly as a panellist in the BBC Radio 4 programme *Any Questions?*. Towards the end of the programme, after the fierce reactions to social or political questions, there comes the opportunity for the panel to relax. The atmosphere is lightened and everyone feels safe again. The panel is asked futile questions which test their inventiveness. Imagination is relegated to lighthearted jest and fun.

But without imagination there would be no longing and no desire to believe that the universe has a human face. And there would be no impulse to help our planet become a home for all, so that all can find justice, beauty and peace in union with God. Our imagination helps us to deal with reality.

The language we use to interpret the world is crucial. Through a variety of images, metaphors, pictures and stories, we begin to make sense of our experience. And those intimations of God and God's world which agitate the human spirit will help us to see, feel and act differently. It is a latent capacity in every person, but especially in the artist, the poet, the composer, the film-maker, the sculptor, the clown. They help us feel again and experience everything that there is to be experienced.

These unarmed prophets may give public voice to the pain, grief and suffering of those whose cries we do not wish to hear. In what appears to be a way of life, a culture which is enduring and resilient, these artists draw attention to the frailty of what seems to be invincible. The root of their criticism is that what seems eternal is in fact fragile, and failing. Such art has a properly subversive quality. It keeps the present provisional and refuses to make it absolute. Powerful regimes of any sort want to ensure that the future is only an unquestioned continuation of the present. The artist says otherwise, and in the dismantling of ideologies and idolatries, suggests and desires another future, for only God is absolute.

In the Christian tradition this has happened time and again by mining the memories of communities, drawing on symbols of saving and redemptive power. Thus, out of the pain and grieving, and the acknowledging of endings (even the ending of death), newness comes and energy is released.

I would like to end this chapter by telling a story which illustrates where that desire and longing are to be found and where hope can be born. It is a story of people on the margins of society. It took place in Philadelphia. I had been visiting churches in different parts of America. They were mostly wealthy, suburban Episcopal churches. But Philadelphia was quite different.

I went to a celebration of the Eucharist arranged by a group called Dignity, which aims to support Catholic homosexual men. There were 200 people in an Episcopal Church Hall – mostly young men in their twenties and thirties. The priest told me afterwards that as far as the Archdiocese of Philadelphia was concerned they were all dead. They were not considered fit to worship in a Roman Catholic Church. That was why they met in a hall and not a church. Yet it was one of the most hopeful, energising celebrations I have ever attended.

There were plenty of tears, particularly at the time of Intercessions when a name was called out, invariably of someone very ill with Aids or perhaps someone who had just died. The congregation responded by saying '*Presente*' (as Chilean mothers have done regularly in Santiago for their husbands and sons who have 'disappeared'). Thus, a strong solidarity between the living, the dying, the sick, the healthy and the dead was expressed. There was anger too, as people told of their experience of prejudice and bigotry.

But the celebration was hopeful. It expressed a desire for justice, wholeness and peace for themselves, their church and the world. Most of those people had experienced or were about to experience loss, and brokenness and pain, yet they could strongly – and with much tenderness and longing – affirm that God was with them. For those men – scorned, rejected, marginalised and persecuted – their faith made sense.

3

CREATION AS
THE BODY OF GOD

This chapter proposes a new way of perceiving God, as one intimately part of all Creation, so intimate that it is possible to speak of Creation as the body of God. But the power of such a metaphor can only be felt in the context of the traditional view of God. This traditional view is the one I grew up with, and it has lingered on into adult life.

I was brought up to believe that God was almighty and omnipotent. To me, an omnipotent being meant someone who could do anything. He could control everything that happened in the present as well as in the future. His all-seeing eyes were literally everywhere. The destiny of the universe was in his strong hands.

As I grew older I became conscious of the presence of evil in the world. Like many others, I had difficulty in squaring evil with a God who was not only powerful but entirely good. I learnt that there were all sorts of arguments to explain evil. The most well known was 'sin'; sinners tended to mess things up, spoiling ourselves and Creation. I have since noticed that many of the explanations of evil have been put together to keep the goodness of God intact! That is to say, God is all good, so we are entirely responsible for evil.

Thus, I knew God as Almighty, King and Lord. When I was a child he was rather like a stern, elderly relative who I was regularly but unwillingly forced to love and placate. I was told we were all his children who had become rebellious through our failure to be obedient to him. Because of this disobedience his Son had been sent as a sacrifice. By his death, salvation and a place in heaven had been procured for us, if we behaved ourselves.

Over time, this view was slightly modified. God was no longer seen as a fierce God, but as a benevolent, parental, all-powerful God who did not want his children to suffer. As the picture filled out, it became considerably more sophisticated, especially in the many complex explanations about what the Son achieved and how he achieved it. In some form or another, this picture has remained with me, and I suspect with many whose allegiance to Christianity tends to be shaky and fitful.

It is an attractive picture of great power, the power of God the Father, contrasting with our own impotence. It is a perception which evokes awe and gratitude to God. There is also a sense of security as I acknowledge my sins before him, and experience a swing from guilt to relief, knowing my sins have been taken away. No one should underestimate the authority and power of this vision, especially those, like myself, who seek to remove it and propose other pictures. It has had strange staying power, which Handel, in his Halleluiah chorus, vividly illustrates:

> For the Lord God Omnipotent reigneth – King of Kings,
> Lord of Lords, for ever, and for ever. Amen.

So much of this picture has permeated our consciousness, that it seems to be an authoritative, definite statement of the way things are. It is almost the foundation of our religion. Indeed, the picture has been worked out carefully and deliberately for 1000 years within Judaism and then Christianity. Ian Barbour describes its development like this:

> The *monarchical model* of God as King was developed systematic-ally, both in Jewish thought (God as Lord and King of the Universe), in medieval Christian thought (with its emphasis on divine omnipotence), and in the Reformation (especially in Calvin's

insistence on God's sovereignty). In this portrayal of God's relation to the world, the dominant western historical model has been that of the absolute monarch ruling over his kingdom.[1]

I now find this way of speaking about God grim, oppressive and unsatisfactory in every way. Investing God with such power has led to the Church supporting Fascism, Nazism and other types of totalitarianism. Thus, God as Lord is brought in on the side of the state to bring their enemies down.

The opposite view is that God is benevolent and will not allow his children to suffer, especially those who obediently abdicate responsibility for their lives to him. This benevolent God, who is still in control, is the God of much popular Christianity. I experienced the full impact of such a God in North-West Texas ('panhandle country' as it is known) in a medium-sized town called Amarillo. In Amarillo all nuclear weapons in the USA are temporarily stored and assembled at Pantex, a company operated for the government by a contractor. From there these weapons are carried by train and truck to military installations all over the country, and beyond – to American bases in Britain and Europe.

Religion thrives in Amarillo. There are at least 190 Protestant churches, 10 Catholic, one Jewish and one Ba-hai community. The Fundamentalist churches are the most prosperous and prominent, and they are growing. The First Baptist Church has more than 10 000 members. Everywhere religion makes its presence felt. In a garage, in Grand Street, I saw a notice saying 'Jesus Christ is King of Kings. Autos serviced'.

The religion of these Texan Christians is simple. They are enthralled by the prospect of Armageddon, believing that they are the final generation, facing inevitable nuclear war, and subsequent nuclear winter. This, they say, will be the great tribulation. At a decisive moment, the believers will be 'raptured' into heaven. The rest – liberals, socialists, all other so-called Christians, non-believers and especially communists – will be burnt and die. They meet to pray to the Lord, study the Bible and become absorbed in the life of their church – easy enough to do with a highly organised social life – coffee mornings, gyms, saunas and the like. They believe Christianity has failed to save the world. Instead they wait eagerly for the return of Jesus Christ – in a state of deferred time – surrounded by godless people, sustained by the Word of God.

Texan Christians, like many others in the USA, Britain and Europe, increasingly live like this in the face of the nuclear threat. It is disturbing and chilling, for the God they worship merely encourages despair as to the possibility of human beings doing anything about their own precarious situation. The God they worship is a God who is Lord and King. He is a distant and remote God who seemed to create the world effortlessly as if he were holding great reserves of power. Once the world had been created that was it. God retreated to his kingdom. The world was too humble to be his royal abode. Occasionally, and dramatically, the distant God would intervene. Speaking about Jesus Christ, David Jenkins, the Bishop of Durham, examines the idea of an interventionist God:

> What sort of God are we portraying and believing in if we insist on what I will nickname 'the divine laser-beam' type of miracle at the heart and basis of the incarnation and resurrection . . . God, it is apparently alleged, works uniquely and directly in a divine intervention on physical matter in order to bring about his basic saving miracles of incarnation and resurrection.[2]

This drama of salvation is played out against the neutral stage of Creation. Nature provides a setting but is neutral in so far as it has no part to play in the drama. Even so, our treatment of Nature is characterised by arrogance and human chauvinism. The American theologian Thomas Berry highlights the dualism between God and Creation which is found in this type of Christianity:

> Human society is not an abstraction. The only real society is the complete society of the natural world. We are awkward at this manner of thinking because our religion as well as our humanist tradition carry a certain antagonism towards the natural world. But now the refusal of human beings to become intimate members of the community of the earth is leading to their own destruction.[3]

One of the reasons for this arrogance is that there is no relationship between the authoritarian, patriarchal God and the
world. There is just a blank. There is nothing about Nature in
this version of Christianity, so she can be destroyed and mutilated. In a religion which speaks so much about the Word of
God, how can the rocks, oceans, trees, animals, birds and
insects, the hills and Earth itself respond to the Word? They can
neither understand nor respond to it. Since Creation is mute,
aggression towards Nature easily follows. It is part of the way
we take things for granted. Nature is there to be conquered,
subdued and mastered.

This picture of God the Father is unsatisfactory. Firstly,
because the traditional views about God are strongest among
the Protestant white middle classes, it excludes women, black,
brown and yellow people. This type of exclusion cannot be limited by just swapping ancient names for God with new ones.
For to put a new name to God is to explore the relationship
between God and the world in a different way – as I will show
when considering God as mother.

Secondly, the traditional picture of God reinforces the
notion that we are all isolated individuals working out our own
individual salvation. Even the Amarillo Christians – for all their
talk of families and fellowship – experience a highly individualistic, private ritual at their baptism. Such a God does not
encourage his puny subjects to take any responsibility except to
follow their own personal paths to heaven.

Given then that this almighty all-powerful God takes no
interest in Nature, how are we to speak about God's relationship to us in a world where there is a burgeoning sense of
humanity occupying one world – a global village? For there is
no point in perpetuating a religion which offers a distant God,
encourages hierarchies, dualism and individualism, and re-
moves any sense of responsibility we hold for one another and
Creation.

If Christianity is to make sense in our own day, different pictures need to be formed which resonate with our deepest
anxieties, fears and aspirations. This is not a superficial desire

to accommodate religion to particular trends and fashions but an attempt to bring into being a Christianity that is not only relevant but resonant.

Relevance is a problem, especially for the clergy, who are frequently accused of this sort of facile accommodation. Most clergy, as they reflect on their ministry, can recall gruesome stories of their attempts at 'outreach' and 'relevance'. (I remember, as a young curate running a youth club, trying to turn the theme song of *Match of the Day* into a hymn tune for our pop group to play at a youth service.) It is not a 'relevant' Christianity that is required but one which embraces our questions, our certainties and our hopes.

Relevance is not the right word. Resonance is. If there are aspects of the gathered experience of nearly 2000 years of Christianity which echo, resonate or strike chords with what is significant today, then ancient metaphors about God will be revitalised or new ones will come into being. However, care has to be taken so that these new metaphors do not become fixed like the authoritarian, patriarchal ones they have replaced. Once a metaphor is fixed, it exercises a tyranny over the imagination and the mind.

One safeguard against this is to ask these questions: Are these pictures on the side of God, life, fulfilment and love which enable us to make sense of our experience? Are they attractive, convincing, surprising, yet familiar? Do they stand being probed and contemplated, but not broken down, analysed, translated or reduced? And, of course, there is the question of truth. It is unavoidable.

In the courtyard of St James's Church, Piccadilly, there is an outdoor pulpit. In the early years of this century, an enterprising rector with a loud voice thought he could evangelise the crowds from this pulpit as they came down Piccadilly. Unfortunately, his voice was drowned out by the clatter of coaches and trams.

Now it is in use again. Each summer, at lunchtime, 'Soap Box' takes place. I use the occasion to make a public exploration of Christianity. On this particular day I was trying out new

ways, models, and approaches in 'seeing' God. I had talked of
God as an artist, servant, mother, lover and companion. Afterwards, a man came up to me and said, 'Your sermon was most
interesting. Once I was a Christian. I think what you are doing
is substituting one myth for another. You have not dealt with
the questions about truth.'

He is right of course. But ultimately the only way I can
answer him is like this: I do not know who God is, in the sense
that I know what a chair is like. I do know that what matters to
me most is love experienced in its many forms – the love of a
mother or father, of a friend or lover. These basic relationships
contain the possibility of glimpsing God's love through these
earthly loves. All the language we use about God is metaphorical. It is, we say, as if God were like this, that or the other. It is
always, strictly speaking, improper and inadequate. God is and
remains a mystery. There are hints, clues and experiences
which point to the nature of God. But they are, in themselves,
too thin and too fragile to form the basis of a mighty philoso-
phy. I am advocating a more personal view of truth: I try to live
by it at whatever cost, but there is always a chance that my con-
jectures about God may not be true.

There is, of course, a more pragmatic question. Do the pictures which emerge illuminate our situation and lead us to a
coherent view of the world today? If they do, it seems sensible
to use them. At least until we find more suitable metaphors.

I want to suggest a picture which stresses God's involvement
with, and commitment to, the Earth – that is to perceive the
Earth as the dwelling place and self-expression of God. It is as if
the Earth is the body of God. Such a view raises the hackles of
many theologians who may say that it reduces God to the level
of the world, destroying his transcendence, and is nothing
more than pantheism and Nature worship. To which I would
reply that God, in this picture, is inclusive of the world but this
is not the sum total of God's reality. For instance, each of us is a
body. But we are more than our bodies; we can choose, consider and reflect. When a person offers his life as a sacrifice for
another, or for a cause, the body is transcended. In the same

way, God is not identified exclusively and ultimately with the world. The Christian tradition has always spoken of the unchanging character of God, and the love of God is not exhausted by the sharing and giving of himself to Creation.

There are many questions about evil, sin, salvation and atonement which look different in the light of this breathtaking and awesome perception that we are literally always and every-where in the presence of God. The point is that we should at least give this idea a chance, as it has great inspirational value.

In searching for some picture less arrogant, less one-dimensional, less tired, less humanly chauvinistic, more cosmic, yet more of the Earth, I have been drawn first to the mystics and poets. Julian of Norwich, in the fourteenth century, wrote of the goodness and closeness of God:

> Our Lord showed me a spiritual sight of his homely and familiar love. I saw that he is everything that is good and comforting to us; he is our clothing – wrapping and enfolding us. He embraces and encloses us in tender love, and he never leaves us. I saw that he is everything that is good, and I understood it. He showed me a little thing, the size of a hazelnut, lying in the palm of my hand, as round as a ball. I looked at it and thought, 'What can this be?' and I was answered, 'It is all that is made.' I wondered how it could last, for I thought that being so small it might suddenly fall apart. And I was answered in my understanding, 'It lasts, and always will, because God loves it.' And so everything has its being through the love of God.
>
> In this little thing I saw three properties. The first is that God made it; the second is that God loves it; the third is that God preserves it. But what is that to me? It is that God is the creator, the lover and protector. For until I am united to him I cannot know love or rest or true happiness; that is until I am so at one with him that no created thing can come between my God and me.[4]

For Julian of Norwich, in everything we do, even in the most natural of activities, those which involve healthy bowel move-ments, God is close:

> A person walks upright, and the food in her body is shut in as if in a well-made purse. When the time of her need arrives, the purse is opened and then shut again in a most fitting fashion. And it is God

who does this, as it is shown when he says that he comes to us in our humblest needs. For God does not despise what he has made, nor does he disdain to serve us in the simplest natural functions of our body, for love of the soul which he created in his likeness. For as the body is clad in the cloth and the flesh is clad in the skin, and the bones in the flesh, and the heart in the chest, so are we, soul and body, clad and enclosed in the goodness of God.[5]

Then, some 300 years later, more exuberant than Dame Julian, Thomas Traherne wrote in his *Centuries of Meditations*:

Your enjoyment of the world is never right, till you so esteem it, that everything in it, is more your treasure than a king's exchequer full of gold and silver. And the exchequer yours also in its place and service. Can you take too much joy in your father's work? He is himself in everything. Some things are little on the outside, and rough and common, but I remember the time when the dust of the streets were as precious as Gold to my infant eyes, and now they are more precious to the eye of reason.[6]

And William Blake, so conscious of how all Creation reflects the Divine, wrote:

I assert for myself that I do not behold the outward creation, and that to me it is a hindrance and not action. . . . 'What!' it will be questioned, 'when the sun rises do you not see a round disc of fire somewhat like a guinea?' 'Oh no, no . . . I see an innumerable company of the heavenly host crying, "Holy, holy, holy, is the Lord God Almighty."'[7]

For me, Gerard Manley Hopkins' sonnet 'God's Grandeur' best expresses the idea of God in Creation:

The world is charged with the grandeur of God
  It will flame out, like shining from shook foil;
  It gathers to a greatness, like the ooze of oil
Crushed. Why do men then now not reck his rod?
Generations have trod, have trod, have trod;
  And all is seared with trade; bleared, smeared with toil;
  And wears man's smudge and shares man's smell: the soil
Is bare now, nor can foot feel, being shod.[8]

The imagery of electricity, flame and shaken tinfoil suggests incredible brilliance and light: God's grandeur cannot be missed or mistaken. But this grandeur is being destroyed, as the image of the treadmill suggests: 'Generations have trod, have trod, have trod'. Pollution and wilful destruction of Nature have taken over so that man can no longer feel the Earth, no longer sense the grandeur of God in Nature. The Earth is bare and 'dead', and men wear shoes.

The implications of this perception for our own time have to be worked out urgently and practically – against a background of the destruction of the environment, and the ability we now have to blow up the planet. It means recovering a reverence and respect for the Earth. As Thomas Berry says, 'The mystique of the land needs to counteract the destructive industrial mystique.'[9]

In the last 20 years or so, we have had the chance to see ourselves as never before. The reactions of astronauts when they observe our planet are those of wonder, awe and amazement. They sense its fragility, its beauty and the interdependence of all its parts. It is ironic that their words, arising as a result of enormous expense and the very best of our human inventiveness, almost mirror those of a culture dying in America – that of the North American Indians – who know absolutely nothing of modern technology.

Respect for the Earth means that Creation has to become our teacher. Environmentalists have shown many times that our disrespect for the delicate balance of the ecological system produces terrifying disasters which cannot be described just as natural disasters or as acts of God. There are, unfortunately, plenty of examples. For instance, there are appalling annual floods in Bangladesh. Television news shows miles and miles of land under water, people homeless and starving. Epidemics then break out. The pictures are familiar because these disasters are so frequent. The deforestation on the lower ranges of mountains has led to the silting up of rivers, which in turn leads to flooding, made worse by the annual monsoon. The deforestation occurs because the timber industry provides a livelihood for a poor country.

There is no simple, quick solution to the flooding of Bangladesh; deforestation cannot be reversed overnight. Difficult political and economic issues have to be faced. My point is a simple and a very basic one: when Nature is violated, Nature will take her revenge, for respect for the Earth means a recognition of the interdependence of all Creation.

Sallie McFague makes this point when she writes:

> The evolutionary, ecological perspective insists that we are, in the most profound ways, 'not our own'; we belong, from the cells of our bodies to the finest creation of our minds, to the intricate, constantly changing cosmos.... To feel in the depths of our being that we are part and parcel of the evolutionary ecosystem of our cosmos is a prerequisite for contemporary Christian theology.[10]

Our task therefore is to be the caretakers and cultivators of the planet – the body of God. For we must recognise that God has risked much for the planet, and has become dependent on us, and suffers with us. There is a precarious nature about this love which God has for Creation, because such limitless and self-giving love depends for its outcome on our response. It is our actions that determine whether the body of God will be outraged, ravaged, even destroyed, or whether through healing and unity it will reflect the divine radiance.

As far as we know, we alone of all beings have a conscience, and we therefore have to become the conscience of the cosmos. We are God's agents, who can consciously befriend the world. Any perception of Christianity which ignores our responsibility for taking care of the Earth, so that there will be a future for our children, needs to be discarded. It is easy to be mesmerised and intimidated by the scale and vastness of the universe, especially when we consider it as the dwelling place of God! After all, you may think, what significance do I – less than the tiniest speck of dust – have in the scale of things?

If it is possible to develop an imaginative way of seeing ourselves in relation to the whole history of evolution, then it is difficult to be indifferent to our place in Creation. We will see ourselves at the apex of all Creation, and recognise what a privilege it is to be human, and what a responsibility we have to the Creation whose agony and groaning have given us birth. On a

visit to the Grand Canyon, Donald Nicholl described how this
came home to him:

> One spring morning I set out at dawn and walked along the top of
> the Grand Canyon down the steep path that leads to the bottom
> where the Colorado River flows, some 7000 feet below. As you
> descend the Canyon you can observe on its walls layer upon layer
> of the sediments that have formed over millions of years, and you
> can relate those layers to the successive species of living creatures,
> both fauna and flora, that dwelt upon this earth before we
> appeared: permian ferns and crinoids and armour-plated fish.
> Observing the tracks of them in this way you feel a true kinship
> with all those beings, knowing that both they and you traced your
> existence back to that first moment of transcendence when life
> appeared on this earth. And then you start to reflect that the very
> eyes with which you are observing these wondrous evidences are
> themselves the result of millions of years of striving for light, ever
> since the first pin-hole eye appeared on these primitive marine
> creatures, the cephalopods. And you are the beneficiary of all that
> struggle for light, the heir to all that agony. And as you gaze at your
> hands or think of your ears or your tongue, it takes your breath
> away to envisage the innumerable strivings that had to be
> attempted before you could see and touch and hear and taste and
> speak. Had any breakdown in that series of stirrings occurred it
> could have destroyed the possibility for you to see and hear and
> sing. The breakdown was prevented by untiring faithfulness on the
> part of millions of beings. The mere thought of this makes you
> realise what an incredible hard-won privilege it is simply to be a
> human being.[11]

And this consciousness of our place in the timescale of the
universe evokes a proper sense of humility, that we are not alien
beings in a cold world, but the beneficiaries of great riches. We
have, as it were, received gifts from God in co-operation with
all those who have struggled and suffered in handing on to us
this particular form of matter which is the human body. This
process started over 20 million years ago when the universe
first began, and then some four million years later when the
Earth was formed, and humankind emerged.

Two issues arise from the argument so far, each to be considered in more detail later. The first question is, what is an appropriate response to Creation as the body of God? It seems to be

not just responsibility, but delight, pleasure and thanksgiving for God's blessing of everything that has been entrusted to us. Without celebration, the spirit withers and dies; this vision of Creation and our place in it would disappear in the face of all the pressures, preoccupations and idolatries of our times. The second issue is how we are to speak of God if the distant God the Father will not do. If the world is perceived as the self-expression of God, as the primary sacrament, then more intimate pictures present themselves – for example, God as Mother. And it is to this that we now turn.

4 GOD AS MOTHER

To recapitulate the argument so far: I believe the claims of Christianity to make sense of all our experience are true. Christianity, as it is currently expressed through the Church, manifestly does not make sense to many people – and not only to atheists, agnostics and those who are indifferent to religion and religious questions.

It is therefore worth attempting to present the claims of Christianity powerfully and persuasively. The first step is to look at the ideology of materialism in a capitalist culture, which provides the conduit for the idolatry of money. This form of idol-worship has diverted religious energies and aspirations from their true goal.

Furthermore, Christianity has its own internal problems in the way it has talked about God. If the traditional image of God the Father no longer works, and belongs to a bygone age, other directions need to be explored. And this exploration could lead to us speaking of the closeness of God in Creation, for example, and seeing the planet as the body of God.

However, this new picture does not help to answer the question: How then, given that God, the all-powerful, almighty Father, is a remote God and does not relate to Nature, are we to speak of God's relationship to us in a world where there is a growing sense of a single worldwide human community? This

sense of mutuality and shared destiny is balanced by our awareness that we have the capacity to destroy Creation. I believe no
version of Christianity is credible if it ignores both the grace of
mutuality and our capacity for destruction – the ecological and
nuclear threat.

To speak of God – in images, metaphors and stories – is to say
'it is as if' God is this, that or the other; and it is inevitable, given
the depth and importance of our subject, that such pictures of
God will come from what is nearest and dearest to us – namely
those relationships without which there is no meaning, no
security, no joy in our lives. It is therefore legitimate to explore
a way of talking about God as if she were our Mother. It is also
possible to speak of God in impersonal terms (Luther's hymn
'A Mighty Fortress is our God' is an example), but we know
ourselves best, and since humankind is probably the most complex being to have evolved there is a wealth of experience to
draw on as we attempt to compose a picture – or part of a picture – of God, in our own likeness. There is really no other way
to do it. Likewise, if my cat were able to express its belief in
God, presumably he would do it in terms of his own cattiness.

It may be said that in substituting Mother for Father nothing
has changed except the name. After all, should we not have
grown out of talking about God as if he or she were a person
who occasionally interfered in our affairs? To this tough and
simple question I would answer that we do not meet God
unmediated but through other people and through facing up
to our problems. What we know of God (and how little we
know, and how paltry our efforts are at describing what we
know) is embodied in our experience, particularly in the longing for communion and union.

Longing is experienced when there is a tension between what
is, and what could be. That is why the voices of women, of the
poor, of the black community, of homosexuals, of those who
speak on behalf of the pain of the Earth and her creatures, and
all those who are marginalised, need to be heard and heeded.
And despite the sheer weight of suffering and pain and injustice, there is a trust that in the end all will be well. The great

Belgian theologian, Edward Schillebeeckx, in a personal testimony, says he believes:

> there is a power at the heart of things who makes for good and who confronts, judges and absorbs what makes for bad; who is available as Spirit, to support struggles for good, confront the work of evil and to renew people in the struggle, and innovate hopefully.[1]

This is the 'something more' dimension in our experience: the transcendent God who calls us to strive harder, do better, and love more effectively, to reach out beyond ourselves and venture into new areas. And it is in this movement forward that we discover that we are not things or objects, but persons fashioned in the image of God, who calls us to know him or her. Dorothy Sölle expresses this simply: 'The dignity of human beings is the capacity for going beyond what exists. We are only truly alive when we transcend.'[2]

Such power, on the side of life and the call to transcendence, is best expressed in personal terms. And because the response has almost always been in relation to a distant masculine God, it is right to discover how in our own day God may be perceived as one who is close to us, intimate with us, nurturing and sustaining Creation. That means an exploration into some aspects of our primary relationships: mother; father as parent; lover and friend, for a start. Some aspects of these different sorts of love may provide a basis for believing in God today as if she were our mother.

The Goddess actually has a very ancient history. Kenneth Leech writes: 'The Mother Goddess in fact dominates the archeological records of the ancient world.'[3] Every major excavation in Palestine has produced some Goddess figurines. E. O. James, who studied the Mother Goddess in great detail, claimed that there was in fact one Goddess worshipped under many names: 'There can be no doubt that in the very earliest ages of human history, the magic force and wonder of the female was no less a marvel than the universe itself.'[4]

Nevertheless, in the most orthodox form of the Jewish religion, the Great Mother, and feminine and female aspects of

God were excluded. Only males were considered true Israelites. However, there are feminine dimensions of God in the Bible – in some of the Psalms and particularly in Proverbs, Ecclesiastes and the Song of Solomon. Although Jesus of Nazareth respected women more than was customary in the first century, by the time St Paul came to write the Pastoral Epistles (the latest writings in the New Testament) women were to be kept firmly in their place.

The patriarchal nature of Christianity has been studied extensively in recent years, and there is no need to repeat the arguments here. The Church developed a hierarchical structure: God as Father and King; Christ the Son in Glory with the Father; then popes, archbishops, bishops, priests (all men); then laymen and laywomen and children. Women were required to worship a male saviour and as the feminist theologian Rosemary Reuther writes:

> Precisely because it is the central symbol in Christianity, it [the Saviour figure] is also the symbol most distorted by patriarchy. All efforts to marginalise women in the Church and Christian society, to deprive them of a voice, leadership, and authority, take the form of proclaiming that Christ was a male and so only the male can 'image' Christ. Woman, while the passive object of his redeeming work, can never actively represent him as mediator of God's word and deed. If feminist theology and spirituality decide that Christianity is irredeemable for women, its primary reason is likely to be this insurmountable block of a male Christ who fails to represent women.[5]

Very occasionally, however, in Christian history the femininity of God has surfaced, particularly in the thirteenth century, when the image of Jesus as Mother was developed and kept alive in the teachings of the Rhineland mystics: Meister Eckhart, Mechthild of Magdeburg, Hildegard of Bingen and, in England, by Julian of Norwich. Anselm, Archbishop of Canterbury in the eleventh century, wrote some extraordinary poetry, much of it bizarre and androgynous. In his 'Prayer for St Paul', Anselm speaks of Christ as Mother. He uses a favourite image of his and other medieval writers, that of the hen gathering her chicks together, (which is taken from Matthew 23:37: 'O Jerusalem, Jerusalem . . . how often would I have gathered thy children together even as a hen gathereth her chickens under her wings, and ye would not.'):

> And you, Jesus, are you not also a Mother?
> Are ye not the mother who, like a hen,
> Gathers her chickens under her wings?
> Truly, Lord, you are a mother . . .

However, it is in the veneration of Mary, the Mother of Jesus, that the true feminine face of God has been seen most vividly. I first became interested in Mary some years ago when I visited Chartres Cathedral, which is dedicated to her. Until then I had been typical of most non-Catholics – I believed anything which got in the way of worshipping God through Jesus Christ was superfluous. I sensed that 'Mary worship' – the shrines and the relics – was superstitious and mixed up with the worship of fertility goddesses. I had other reservations too. The Church had been run by a hierarchy of men. They were celibate and they had turned Mary into a pure virgin or a symbol of perfect motherhood. Either way this 'worship' degraded women, because their sexuality had been banished.

But then I went to Chartres. There the sublime and the ordinary are close together. If you look at the stained glass, religion and everyday life, farming and the crucifixion, are all mixed together. We are not used to this kind of proximity today. Chartres is not a museum. The building had such a profound effect on me because it made me think that, dedicated as it was to the Mother of God, it must contain something on which all Christians (Catholic and non-Catholic) could build.

In the centre of the west portal is Mary seated on her throne, crowned. She holds the Child. She is, to use an ancient title, the *Theotokos* (the God-bearer). And that is the secret. For me, Mary presents one of the human faces of God. She gives us the chance to experience the quality of God in the person of a woman. She offers healing, warmth and protection: and in her grief expresses something of the God who suffers with us. Mary is the emblem of human sorrow – innocence victimised by injustice. Her heart is pierced by anguish. A mother is silenced by sorrow. That is why the 'Stabat Mater' has inspired so many composers:

> At the Cross her station keeping
> Stood the mournful mother weeping,
> Close to Jesus at the last:
> Oh, how sad and sore distressed
> Was that mother highly blessed
> Of the sole-begotten One!
> Christ above in torment hangs;
> She beneath beholds the pangs
> Of her dying glorious Son.
> Who is he could keep from weeping?
> While he saw the Saviour's mother,
> In such depths of sorrow and distress?
> Can the human heart refrain
> From partaking in her pain,
> In that mother's pain untold?
> Bruised, derided, cursed, defiled,
> She beheld her tender Child
> All with bloody scourges rent;
> For the sins of his own nation,
> Saw him hang in desolation,
> Till his spirit forth he sent.
> O thou mother! Fount of love!
> Touch my spirit from above,
> Make my heart with thine accord:
> Make me feel as thou hast felt;
> Make my soul to glow and melt
> With the love of Christ my Lord.

The difficulty with Marian devotion, as Protestants have been quick to recognise, is that while Mary is the 'bearer of God' she has been endowed with divine attributes, fantastic characteristics and titles. She is not God, but she has been worshipped as if she were. Kenneth Leech quotes the theologian Von Balthasar:

> Without Mariology, Christianity threatens imperceptibly to become inhuman. The Church becomes functionalistic, soulless, a

hectic enterprise without any point of rest, estranged from its true nature by planners. And because, in this masculine world, all that we have is one ideology replacing another, everything becomes polemical, critical, bitter, humourless, and ultimately boring, and people in their masses turn away from such a Church.[6]

In other words, to compensate for a stern, remote, masculine God, the worship of Mary was, if not encouraged, at least tolerated – but this itself leads to a distortion of the nature and being of God, for God is regarded exclusively in masculine terms.

This rapid and incomplete survey of Christian practice and experience has shown that, in spite of psychological, social and political factors, the worship of God as Mother has never disappeared and, particularly in Marian devotion, has flowered at whatever cost to orthodox belief in God. Feminist theologians have used these traditions for their own purposes. But this gathering of past experience is not sufficient. Today it is also necessary to discover what sort of love, what sort of activity, is suggested by proposing God as Mother.

Christians often speak of being 'born again', referring to their spiritual rebirth. Rarely do they acknowledge their physical birth, simply because of the long history of sexual repression and fear of the body. In the new baptism service, for example, there are numerous references to water, but none about the waters released at birth. Yet the experience of 'birthing' is generally perceived as a mystery and a miracle. Giving birth is being part of, and co-creators of, a process in which life is being passed on. To speak of God as Mother is to affirm the holiness and sacredness of the physical (body, blood and water – all matter which makes life possible). God as Mother closes the gap between body and soul, spirit and material, which together with all the other dualisms have blighted institutional religion.

The creation of new life is not, however, confined to women alone. Meister Eckhart says 'All are called to be mothers.' By this he means that the creative energies latent in everyone need to be developed, and released into areas of compassion and celebration. To recognise ourselves in whatever capacity as co-creators is to begin to see our responsibility for helping life along – gardening, farming, teaching, healing, building, writing, painting, making music, working for peace and for justice – these activities are about preserving and continuing life. As creators, our concern is not just to save ourselves, but to bring more life into existence.

If we could allow this simple and neglected affirmation to seep into our consciousness we would begin to overcome our fatalism about the future. It would also help us to become more vigilant about preventing further environmental degradation of the planet, and it would make us face up to the threat of a nuclear catastrophe.

The mother when she first sees her baby may say, 'It is marvellous that you exist, that you are in this world. You are infinitely precious.' Therefore it is not only the birth which is significant, but the continuing process of nurturing and nourishing; nourishing her own children, yes, but also reaching out to include everyone and everything, particularly the weak, the vulnerable and the oppressed. (Here the image of the hen and the chicks is particularly telling.) In speaking of God as Mother, it is easy to identify her with what are generally called feminine qualities – tenderness, gentleness and warmth – and to leave God as Father with his authority, anger and power. But that is to perpetuate the old dualism. In the cult of Mary, we have seen how she is 'created' to offer protection, but she is also Mary of the Magnificat, and the Mother of Justice.

A fresh perception of Mother as Judge has to go alongside the Mother as Nourisher. But the judgement is not the same as that of the masculine King and Lord. There the Judge passes sentence and punishes sinners, or he takes the punishment upon himself and then the sinners are absolved. They are almost passive spectators in their own drama of salvation.

But Mother of Justice is concerned for the welfare of all Creation; her desire is that the entire cosmic household should be ordered in justice and in harmony. Her justice, like her mercy, is inclusive, because the mother has a profound sense of the organic, interrelated, nature of the whole. It is in her, in a world resembling a womb, that we gain a sense of our dependence on

Nature, and realise that we live, move and have our being in
her. A striking illustration of this is the beautiful saying of the
Buddha: 'As a mother with boundless devotion regards her
only child so let us survey the world.'

Perhaps this is becoming too fanciful. I have merely taken a
few steps in exploring what the earthly mother does when she
creates, gives birth and nurtures her child. But within that pattern of creation it may be appropriate to speak of God as Crea-
tor and Mother, at least in some ways and on some occasions
for, like all images of God, it is limited and partial.

A difficult question which emerges from this (and indeed
from all ways of talking about God) is, how should God be
addressed? The trouble with 'O God, our Father and Mother' is
that it easily turns those who pray into children. And the mater-
nal image is designed to encourage responsibility for the Creation, rather than childlike helplessness. Probably what is
needed, particularly in public worship when the name of God
is uttered most, is the use of a great range of names for God.
This would contribute a much-needed richness to our modern
liturgies, in which at present the image of 'Heavenly Father'
reigns alone above all others.

5

JESUS CHRIST –
LIVING WITH QUESTIONS

The discussion in this chapter follows three different paths, but they are interrelated because they are all concerned with questions about our perception and understanding of Jesus Christ. The first path is a consideration of the relationship between Christianity and truth, and in particular how the vociferous and growing body of Christian Fundamentalists regard truth and the Bible. The second raises issues about Jesus, particularly the kind of knowledge we have about him and its extent. And the third suggests a possible response to the question: Who is Jesus Christ for us today?

Christianity and Truth

My grandfather was a Victorian squire. Each morning, so my father remembered, the household gathered in the dining-room for prayers. A Victorian family Bible was open on the table. Some verses were read and my grandfather made a few comments. Prayers were said. Then my grandmother, the children, the housekeeper and the servants dispersed to their duties for the day. Many years later I came across that Bible. It was falling to bits. I asked my father if I could repair it, sell it or if it was of no value throw it away. He was shocked. It had been in the family a long time.

'You should keep it,' he said.

'But no one reads it; what's the point of holding on to it?' I asked.

My father's reluctance to part with the Bible was very strong. There it was, unread, unused, never consulted, gathering dust in the loft. My father was not at all interested in religious matters. He went to church once a year – at Christmas – and that was all. I sensed his reluctance to let the Bible go, partly because it was a talisman, and partly because it held a lot of precious and dwindling memories of his childhood.

But there was a deeper reason: to destroy the Bible was like destroying, finally and ultimately, a very distant landscape which was certainly not part of any contemporary picture, but was still half-consciously a part of the way our attitudes, opinions and feelings had been formed. For centuries the Bible had been regarded not just as a holy book but as an encyclopaedia, a moral 'highway code', a school book for children, the repository of law. It was believed to provide all the necessary information for living – certainly for religious matters, but also for secular matters – science, astronomy, cosmology, economics, politics, history, geography and music.

By my grandfather's time such a view of the Bible had long since disappeared (except perhaps as some sort of folk memory). A new source of knowledge had appeared which challenged the truth of authoritative, revealed religion in the Word of God – science. And this new knowledge was heralded by advances in the science of astronomy. Galileo's observation – through his telescope – confirmed the Copernican assertion that the Earth revolved round the sun. But the Bible said that the Earth was still, and the sun and the stars moved round the Earth. The Earth had always been regarded as the centre of the universe. Galileo tried to show that there was confirmation for the Copernican system in the Bible.

Bertolt Brecht's play *Life of Galileo* is less concerned with theological matters and more with Galileo as the 'champion of a new spirit of empiricism and untrammelled scientific enquiry and the Church as the defender of the faith'.[1] But Brecht nevertheless makes the point that the new knowledge does not just threaten the old order, but brings to an end its hierarchical, authoritarian aspect. The Ballad Singer takes up Galileo's new ideas in Scene 10:

> When the Almighty made the universe
> He made the earth and then he made the sun.
> Then round the earth he bade the sun to turn –
> That's in the Bible, Genesis, Chapter One.
> And from that time all creatures here below
> Were in obedient circles meant to go.
>
> So the circles were all woven:
> Around the greater went the smaller
> Around the pace-setter the crawler
> On earth as it is in heaven.
> Around the pope the cardinals
> Around the cardinals the bishops
> Around the bishops the secretaries
> Around the secretaries the aldermen
> Around the aldermen the craftsmen
> Around the craftsmen the servants
> Around the servants the dogs, the chickens and the beggars.[2]

Galileo is significant, because he was almost the first (and certainly the most notorious) representative of a long list of those who have had to square the results of their curiosity and fervent enquiry into reality with their religious beliefs. In Galileo's case, the difficulty was trying to resolve a basic contradiction between the Bible – an entirely accurate, revealed source of truth – and what had been discovered.

In 1615 Galileo wrote to Christina, Grand Duchess of Tuscany, to resolve the problem. John Bowden, in *Jesus: The Unanswered Questions*, writes that Galileo's open letter 'has been said to be one of the most remarkable documents in the history of biblical criticism'. He summarises Galileo's position:

> Scripture and nature both proceed from the word of God, but nature is inexorable and immutable, whereas the Bible often speaks figuratively to accommodate itself to human understanding. Once evidence emerges in the scientific sphere as to a particular state of affairs, that must be accepted; the authority of the Bible may not be

made binding on scientific questions. But Galileo pleads for a
recognition of the differences between knowledge which has a
demonstrable basis, which does not depend on interpretation, and
knowledge over which argument is legitimately possible, where
interpretation is involved. There is no way of suppressing this one
kind of truth, whether by silencing individuals, banning books or
even prohibiting the study of authority altogether. Even the Pope
is powerless here.[3]

The Church's response is well known. Galileo was condemned
by the Inquisition in 1633; he recanted and died a broken man.

Unfortunately, that has generally been the response of the
Church to those who seek to be Christian, but are also driven to
search out the truth by means of scientific observation, experiment and analysis. In Galileo's day, attempts were made to
describe new discoveries in ways which did not challenge or
contradict the Bible. But those days are long past. Now the via-
bility of religious belief has to be tested and refined in the light
of our knowledge of the universe, of evolution, of the whole
complex organism of the planet, and of historical changes.

Galileo had little chance of redress. Many had already been
imprisoned, tortured and burnt at the stake for their views.
Others have suffered in an altogether milder way, putting up
with vilification and harassment or being forced to resign from
their university posts. In the nineteenth century such a list
would have included the theologians David Strauss, F. D.
Maurice, Robertson Smith, Alfred Loisy and the Jesuit George
Tyrrell. Today's roll call includes the theologians Teilhard de
Chardin, Hans Küng, Edward Schillebeeckx, Leonardo Boff,
Jacques Pohier, Matthew Fox, Charles Curran and Archbishop
Hunthausen. All these men have been 'disciplined', 'threat-
ened', 'investigated' or 'silenced' by the Vatican.

The Anglican Church's limits of toleration are considerably
broader than the contemporary Roman Catholic Church, but
the views of the late Bishop John Robinson, the Reverend Don
Cupitt and Bishop David Jenkins of Durham have encountered
highly critical reactions and attempts to ridicule and even
marginalise them so that they could be readily discounted.

Little has changed since Galileo's day. The fundamental issues remain the same.

Writing in the *Church Times*, after the media's response to his comments on the notorious *Credo* television programme in which he expressed his views on the virgin birth and resurrection, the Bishop of Durham Elect, as he was then, wrote:

> Apostolic and missionary responsibilities for the Christian faith demand, not the defence of credal formulae, but the exploration and exposition of the great Catholic symbols in the light of the best current knowledge and the deepest contemporary experience . . .

> Nearly 50 years of conscious Christian discipleship and well over 30 years of passionate study and teaching at all levels and in many places have convinced me that facing the issues of critical study, historical knowledge and scientific thinking are essential to our mission to our believing and would-be believing fellows.[4]

That the Bishop of Durham was compelled to write in such a manner shows just how repressive our religious institutions have become. Even allowing for the media hype, reactions to the Bishop of Durham's statements indicate a Church suffering from a form of corporate depression, where enquiry, questions and wrestling with issues of faith are not allowed in public. Of course, it has been argued that the raising and exploring of questions, the airing of doubts, is fine for professors in the senior common room, but a bishop's job is to preserve unity, and teach the faith. He should not cause havoc, by undermining the simple faith of ordinary people.

To argue that the pursuit of truth is best left to academics and that raising questions is destructive and disruptive is both blasphemous and patronising. It is blasphemous because if God is a God of truth, then, as Galileo reminded the Pope, truth will not be stopped wherever that search may lead. (The history of Christianity has shown that truth cannot be suppressed.) Such arguments are also patronising because they imply that each Christian is an 'ordinary person' with a 'simple faith'.

In more than 25 years as a priest I have never met such a person. It is insulting to underestimate anyone's ability to engage in thoughtful and often difficult and painful rethinking of attitudes and opinions. Where those opportunities and forums are created vitality is generated, which, of course, is the last thing that a depressed institution wants.

At St James's Church, we have experienced this vitality from time to time. Several times a year the form of the sermon is changed. Instead of the preacher speaking to a mute audience, there is an opportunity for everyone to participate. The sermon takes place at the end of the liturgy. The preacher speaks for some minutes and the congregation have a chance to consider what has been said by talking to one another. Then questions are asked, either of each other, or the preacher, and the process is repeated two, three or four times. The preacher then invites written or verbal comments which assist him in preparing next week's sermon. Many who have taken part in these events have experienced a new freedom of the spirit. And through attentive listening, they have gained insights and begun to change.

The only rule is that everyone's opinions are respected as they would wish their own to be. For myself I have discovered over the years that the better I am at learning, the better I become at teaching. Yet what I am describing is rare today. A closed-minded Church has been made even narrower by the growth of Fundamentalism, and something must be said about this phenomenon, not least because its adherents would prob-ably say that most of this book is of the devil itself!

Fundamentalism has its roots in the Evangelical Revival of the nineteenth century. In contrast to the drab, austere formal-ism of Victorian religion, the Revivalists preached a particular religious experience: namely, the opportunity of repentance and salvation through the cleansing blood of Christ on the cross. The certainty this generated meant a warm, lively and secure religion.

Fundamentalists have always attacked 'nominal' Christians; they profess Christ yet they are false. They say nominal Chris-tians are wishy-washy about the Bible, and that they will get to heaven by their own efforts, and hesitate about Jesus being God. These 'false' liberal nominal Christians are the real target of Fundamentalist Christians. Because they are aware that

'Fundamentalism' is not an attractive description, they invariably describe themselves as Conservative Evangelicals, and are
found both in separate churches and in the mainstream
denominations.

For the Fundamentalist, the question of truth has been
decided. It lies in the Bible. The Bible, they say, is inspired
because it says so. Fundamentalists do not, as is often said,
believe the Bible is to be taken literally. But they believe that it
is inerrant – that it is completely correct and without mistakes.
To preserve inerrancy, interpretation varies between the symbolic and the literal. Few would interpret the account of the
Creation in Genesis 1 literally; rather, it was a way of saying that
God made everything.

On the other hand, when it suits them, literal interpretations
are adopted. Thus, the virgin birth has to be understood literally because it preserves the strong Fundamentalist belief that
Jesus Christ is unique – God was effectively walking about in a
man's body in Jesus. The virgin birth provides a litmus test for
the authority of scripture; and to deny the virgin birth is to
deny the deity of Christ.

Fundamentalists expend a lot of energy ensuring that all the
events in the Bible harmonise. Nothing must disturb its
inerrancy. Thus, in Matthew, Mark and Luke, the cleansing of
the Temple takes place at the end of Jesus's ministry; in St John
it takes place at the beginning. The *New Bible Commentary
(Revised)* says, 'By far the most satisfactory solution is that Jesus
cleansed the Temple twice.' Such absurdities are the most con-
venient way of dealing with contradictory accounts of the same
event happening on different occasions.

This flat-footed approach is accompanied by others. For
example, they employ the most up-to-date scientific knowledge to preserve the integrity of biblical stories. In his classic
critique, *Fundamentalism*, James Barr illustrates this from
Bernard Ramm's account of the flood (in *The Christian View of
Science and Scripture*). Ramm ignores the possibility that Noah's
flood may be a myth:

The question then is whether the flood was a universal flood, covering the whole earth or, as many conservative interpreters hold, a local Mesopotamian flood. The latter is Ramm's own opinion. Many powerful arguments support this case. The highest mountain in the Mesopotamian area was Ararat, about 17,000 feet. But the Himalayas rise to 29,000 feet. The amount of water required to provide a universal flood, covering the Himalayas and all the rest of the world, would be very great, 'about eight times more water than we now have'. God would have had to perform a special creation of water to furnish this much, but the scriptures give no hint of such a special creation. Equally difficult would be the problem of getting rid of all this water. The Bible makes it clear that the waters of the flood were removed by draining them away, but 'If the entire world were under six miles of water, there would be no place for the water to drain off'. A local flood would readily dispose of the problem. Again, devastating effects would have been exercised on marine life both by the mixing of fresh and salt water and by the enormous pressure of such a depth of water. Plant life would have suffered too: 'practically the entire world of plants would have perished under the enormous pressure, the presence of salt water, and a year's soaking'. Again, there would have been a multitude of difficulties connected with the animals, if the flood was a universal flood. How did the animals get from distant lands to the ark? Kangaroos, llamas and polar bears would presumably have had to make the long journey to Mesopotamia. There is no doubt that God could arrange this, but it seems doubtful whether this is really intended by the scriptural record. Again, after the flood was over, all these animals, two by two, would have had to get back to Australia, South America and so on. An accident to only one of any species would have meant the complete extinction of that species. 'Once in the ark, the problem of feeding and caring for them would be enormous. The task of carrying away manure and bringing food would completely overtax the few people in the ark.' For these and similar reasons one should favour the view of a purely Mesopotamian flood.[5]

Most Conservative Evangelicals do not bother themselves with these matters although, as James Barr points out, many commentators take Ramm's line. But the fact remains that the purpose of all these 'intellectual gymnastics' is to preserve the inerrancy of the Bible – for, give an inch, and the whole edifice collapses:

> If you allow a man to say that Deuteronomy is from a long time
> after Moses, then next he will be saying that Jesus never said the
> things he is reported in the Gospels to have said, and from this it is
> but a short step to saying that Jesus never existed, or that the patri-
> archs were moon-gods, or that St Paul totally misunderstood the
> actual message and place of Jesus.[6]

In any long-term view, Fundamentalist Christianity has no
future. Its intellectual base is quite inadequate to sustain a ref-
ormation of the Church. But its power and the certainty and
security it offers are a growing feature of religious life in Europe
and the USA. It is difficult to have discussions with such people. The divide between 'nominal' and 'true' Christians is central to their system of belief: it is pointless to invite them to be
more open or understanding. They operate with a strong sense
of group loyalty, which does not tolerate or invite outsiders. It
is necessary to understand what Fundamentalism is about, to
point out quietly and carefully that their beliefs are unhelpful
and limited. As and when people move away from Fundamentalism (partly because it is a very immature and repetitive form
of religious belief), then there should be opportunities for 'de-
briefing'. Otherwise, as I have found, there are those who live
with absolutely unnecessary guilt feelings for the rest of their
lives or give up the practice of religion altogether.

This rapid survey of some aspects of Christianity and truth
has been undertaken to provide a framework for the next part
of this chapter – an exploration of the person of Jesus, and the
Gospels which provide all the information we have about him.
One of the inevitable results of studying, say the Gospels, as
one would study any other ancient text, with all the rigour of a
historian, scientist or literary critic, is to realise that the world of
Palestine 2000 years ago was quite different from ours.

Jesus and the Gospels

My conversion to Christianity had nothing to do
with the Bible, nor with the person of Jesus Christ. It began as a

prompting from God, which became so persistent that I could not ignore it. The first thing I did on becoming a Christian was to read the Gospels, and start going to church. I remember all those years ago, the effect the Gospels had on me. To read the Gospels was to be confronted with what struck me as a set of impossible demands. If I was to be a true disciple I had to break from my family, give up everything and take on a life of itinerant insecurity. Time and again I picked up the warnings about money being an obstacle to salvation. I was to try and become a forgiving and gentle person, straining after a new form of justice where the rich were 'sent away' and the poor raised up. And I had to be prepared to put up with division, opposition, persecution, even death, for the sake of Jesus Christ.

On the other hand, the congregation I joined was concerned with raising money for a new roof, building up a choir, and organising themselves into groups for studying the Gospels I had just been reading. There seemed to be no link between the radicalism of the Gospels, and the preoccupations of that congregation.

But I found the Gospels unhelpful. By becoming a Christian I had hoped that God would help me to become a better person; but there were no guidelines, just these incredible requirements and promises which seemed idealistic, utopian and quite unreachable! Thus, the Gospels seemed unhelpful on how precisely I should live out my life.

They were also amazingly familiar. A public school education with a lot of enforced attendance of chapel services had made me half-familiar with the parables and stories about Jesus. I caught the radicalism of Jesus's demands, and yet found the Gospels uninteresting – not a promising start for a new Christian. And then, the Gospels (and much of the rest of the Bible as I came to read it) had a somehow one-dimensional quality – strange, unhelpful, familiar, monochrome.

But once I started to read and study the Gospels carefully with the aid of 'Galileo's successors' (experts on historical and literary criticism) everything changed. It was as if a veil had been lifted and my imagination was inspired to make connections between what I was learning about the Jesus of history and the world today.

This is what I learnt: I discovered that Mark's was the first Gospel; where he got his material from no one really knows. Matthew and Luke used a lot of Mark, but added another source of sayings of Jesus. John was written later. Matthew and Luke often changed what Mark had written for their own purposes. Matthew and Luke also diverge a great deal in their accounts of the birth and resurrection. These differences and divergences were, I learnt, inevitable because the three Gospel writers were in effect editors. They gathered stories about Jesus, like 'pearls on a string' into the Gospels. Because of the gaps, contradictions and divergences in the Gospels, the 'lives of Jesus' are inevitably coloured by the authors' prejudices and assumptions.

I discovered, too, that there were at least three distinct phases in the New Testament. The first was the Jewish Palestinian phase in which Jesus, recognisably Jewish, led an itinerant life, moving from place to place with his disciples, telling whoever would listen that they were living at a time of great crisis and God's kingdom had arrived. This period ended with his death.

The second phase grew out of the experience of the resurrection when settled Christian communities sprang up in Turkey and Greece. The religion was so attractive that churches quickly came into being, not least because of the expectation that the world would soon come to an end. Many of St Paul's letters were written in this middle phase. It offered salvation, through the death of Jesus Christ. And at this stage the Christian religion makes the transition from its beginnings in a rural backwater in a minor Syrian province, virtually indistinguishable from any other Jewish sect, to a full-scale religion of universal appeal with all the sophisticated trappings of Greek culture.

Lastly, another phase is discernible. As the prospect of the world ending receded, so the members of the early Church had to conform to the world in which they found themselves, as respectable, law-abiding citizens. This 'respectability' is found

in the letters of Timothy and Titus attributed to Paul, but probably written by others.

Discovering the background of the New Testament (and of
the Old as well) removed the one-dimensional impression that
it had made on me when I first started to read it. The irritating
sense of half-familiarity quickly vanished. Instead I became
aware of the strangeness of the world of the Gospels. It was
believed that the world was created in six days about 75 generations before their own day. They believed God to be firmly in
control of the world. While he allowed life to follow a generally
ordered pattern – day and night, and the cycle of the seasons –
he occasionally intervened and revealed his power, either
through natural events like earthquakes, or through miracles.
Miracles were regarded as divine signs rather than a breach of
natural law.

God was not, however, the only supernatural being. Demons
and angels were everywhere. Demons invaded the body, and
were the cause of every sort of illness and mood. Angels, however, could bring good desires, and guidance and wisdom
pleasing to God. The world was regarded as a battleground
between the forces of good and evil.

People believed that the world would end soon with an
assumed victory for God. He would bring everything to an end,
and begin a new state of affairs called the Age to Come. Many
were impatient for this end, and could not understand why
God was delaying. Perhaps, they thought, it was because everyone needed time to repent, since only the chosen were going to
enjoy God's new order. Or they may have believed that there
was going to be terrible suffering, and a fierce struggle between
good and evil just before the end came. Some believed that
Jesus had won the first round in the battle against evil, particularly during the time he spent in the wilderness which was
believed to be the home of the demons.

The supernatural is conveyed throughout the Gospels, not
just in the miracles – those of healing or the more startling ones
where Nature is obedient to the will of God – but also in the
language. For the New Testament writers, words readily con-

veyed different levels of meaning. For example, much has been written about the star which rose to herald the birth of Jesus and guided the wise men in their search to find him. The German astronomer Kepler in the early seventeenth century thought it was a supernova – a new star which a distant star explodes so that for a short period of time it gives out a great deal of light. Others have said that it was a planetary conjunction between Jupiter and Saturn. The evidence for these different explanations is most inconclusive. On the other hand, not so many commentators have noticed that the births and deaths of great men were traditionally marked by heavenly signs. The readers of St Matthew's Gospel, where the star is mentioned, would have had no difficulty in recognising its significance.

The strangeness of this remote world certainly makes teaching and preaching about Jesus Christ exacting; it calls for much imagination to move readily from our world to that of first-century Palestine. And there are limits to our ability to enter the minds of people from a different culture. Louis MacNeice wrote these lines about the ancient Greeks: 'The dead are dead/ And how one can imagine oneself among those I do not know./ It was all so unimaginably different and all so long ago.'[7] In other words, it is impossible for us to become first-century Palestinian Jews.

But other difficulties began to surface, some of which I have already suggested. One was the variety and diversity of the forms of Christianity which appear in the New Testament. I had been brought up to believe that the growth of the early Church was a smooth, successful and uniform development. But I soon discovered this was not so. Robert L. Wilken, in *The Myth of Christian Beginnings*, says:

There is no original Christian faith, no native language, no definitive statement of the meaning of Christ for all times. The dialectic of past and present, tradition and innovation, permanence and change, runs through the whole history of Christianity. What is regarded as novel to one generation becomes authoritative tradition to another. Christians have, in their construction of the past, prized antiquity, stability, and permanence, but the historical record shows us quite another picture. Christians have said one thing while going ahead and doing something else. The apostles spoke several languages, and Christians ever since have done the same. No matter how deeply we probe, how early we extend our search, we will never find an original faith. We can't go home again, not only because the home we once knew has changed beyond recognition. No, there never was a home. From the beginning, Christians have been wanderers and pilgrims whose dream lies not in the past, but before them and all men – in the future.[8]

It is therefore not possible to know precisely what it was that Jesus said or did. Certainty will continue to be elusive.

Much of what I have written about the search for the historical Jesus is kept 'under wraps'. Academics are distrusted for they seem to erode the ground of certainty with their persistent and unwavering search for truth. At theological colleges and seminaries, students preparing for ordination come across the fruits of all this work and research. They may well be told as they learn how to preach to 'take account' of all this 'criticism', as it is technically known, but their real task is to proclaim the Gospel and not to disturb their congregations with all these questions.

I do not believe that it matters that we cannot find a definitive, once and for all, Jesus. Faith is not dependent on such certainties and securities. Moreover, it is just not possible to find the whole of Christian belief and practice in the New Testament. Professor Dennis Nineham, in 'The Strangeness of the New Testament World', writes:

> Christianity may be pictured as a long and wide river of which the New Testament events and teachings were but the source; Cardinal Newman argued interestingly in favour of some such model. Or it may be pictured, for instance, as a growing oak tree which has developed from an acorn but no longer is, or is meant to be, identical with its original form, and may yet grow into forms more different still. Those who work with such an understanding suggest that right from the earliest days, each generation, as it entered upon its Christian heritage, has made adjustments to the gospel where the shoe has pinched, so to speak, where different cultural circumstances have made it necessary. Many of those who have made these changes have been unaware of what they were doing, but the

cumulative effect of their activity has been to make Christianity today something significantly different from the New Testament faith – and none the worse for that.[9]

The earliest Christians tried to work out who Jesus was for them, in their own times. This varied considerably according to whether they lived in Egypt, Syria or Rome, and Christianity has done the same ever since. Of course, to admit this is to be accused of saying that anything goes. Jesus can then be turned into the image of anything or anybody; truth is literally abandoned. But when it is possible to make connections at the deepest level between what we know of Jesus and the Church in the New Testament, and what we experience in our own day, then a demanding, challenging, life-enhancing picture of Jesus Christ emerges. And this picture is of inestimable value in the search for communion with one another, with Creation and with God.

Another generation will make different connections, and perceive reality differently. But that is to be expected. If it is true that the living tradition of Shakespeare's plays can be constantly reinterpreted, then how much more can that be said of Jesus – the founder of Christianity – as seen in the Gospels. Not everything that can be said will be said or understood. What is not clear is best left. Another generation and another time may claim as theirs what is now a mystery for us. We can only do what we are capable of today. And so to the question: Who is Jesus Christ for us today?

Jesus Christ Today

Perhaps I have moved too easily from speaking about Jesus the historical person to Jesus Christ the person of faith. The words Jesus and Christ spring from different worlds: Jesus is the Greek version of the Aramaic and Hebrew name Joshua. Christ is a Greek title for Messiah, and this was the name with which the earliest Greek-speaking community honoured Jesus.

Christ has been honoured in countless ways. If a cursory look at the New Testament does not reveal the richness and diversity of the way Christ has been interpreted, it is not necessary to be an ecclesiastical historian or even a well-informed observer to notice the plethora of Christian denominations. *The World Christian Encyclopedia* (published in 1982) lists 20 800 different Christian denominations, and within those churches there will be a range of perceptions as to what the person of Christ represents. The character of the worship in each church reflects the particular Christ that is worshipped. Experience, for example, the Orthodox Liturgy, a meeting of the Society of Friends, a Catholic Mass in an Austrian village or in the shanty towns by a Brazilian city, a Lutheran morning service in Sweden, a Dutch Reformed service in South Africa, a Black Pentecostal service, let alone – nearer home – the varieties of worship of the English churches, and it is impossible to say, as some evangelists do, with St Paul, that 'Jesus Christ is the same yesterday, today, for ever.'

The works of art which have portrayed Christ down the ages also reveal richness and diversity, from the earliest representations in the catacombs of Christ as a Roman citizen, to those of Jesus enthroned as Emperor in the Ravenna mosaics. From these, one can move on to the splendour of the medieval and Renaissance Christs, to the Victorian Christ, to the contemporary Christ as the Jewish teacher, the clown, the magician, the superstar, the supreme artist, the liberator of the oppressed. The list is endless.

Yet, for all this diversity, significant groups have felt excluded. Black communities perceive the white Christ as an oppressive Messiah, and have created their own black Christ, black Madonna and Child. For them, 'Christ *really* enters into our world where the poor, the despised and the black are, disclosing that he is with them, enduring their humiliation and pain, and transforming oppressed slaves into liberating servants'.[10] The black Christ highlights the incipient and often unspoken racism of the white Christ, for 'white' is not the same as neutral. The white Christ has been consistently used to reinforce the position of the powerful, and the subordination of the weak.

The other group who have felt excluded are women. Christ cannot be a representative for them, since he is male, and they are not. Many women find it impossible to worship a male God, so there have been tentative explorations into images of Christ as female, of which the best known is Edwina Sandy's *Christa* – a crucified woman. This sculpture was hung in a chapel in the Cathedral of St John the Divine in New York, and was the subject of much controversy.

Images like this one are a long way from the Jesus of history, and far from the tradition and experience of the Church until now. But it is important that these issues about the representation of Christ are aired in public and not behind closed doors. Any discussion has to recognise the obvious – that there is absolutely no standard or agreed definitive 'model' of Christ for the whole of Creation to worship. As with the Jesus of history, so with the Christ of the Church; he is created and recreated in our own image.

Before considering the question of who Christ is for us today in Europe, it is necessary to consider the phenomenon of 'liberation theology'. This picture of a Christ of and for the poor has caught the imaginations of millions all over the world. Indeed, the Christ of liberation theology seems to be the most vibrant and living Christ for us today. In 'Where do we go from here?', an article in the Catholic magazine *Concilium*, Samuel Rayan, a Jesuit Professor of Theology in Delhi, writes:

> Jesus lived on this earth, a human being among humans, like us in all things except that he was never closed to reality but wholly open to nature, people and God. He grew in love and became it ever more completely and purely. He identified with the poor and was in solidarity with the oppressed – and discerned the cause of the down-trodden as God's cause in history. Solidarity with the oppressed, solidarity with God – a love that transformed him into itself and is akin to what is deepest and most alive in God. The conclusion is that what is done to the poor and the lowly is done to Jesus – is done to God. That is the orientation of Third World Christology. Four US women were abducted by security forces in

San Salvador and were killed and buried in a cow pasture. Of them Jon Sobrino said: 'Maura, Ita, Dorothy and Jean are Christ dead today'.

But they are also the risen Christ who keeps alive the hope of liberation. Salvation comes from Jesus. Salvation comes through Mary. It comes through all women and men who love truth and love people to the extent of giving their own life. Jesus suffers now, is scourged and crucified now, in Catholic countries, in prisons and slums and mines and plantations. We must rediscover the real presence of Christ in the poor and the continuation of his liberating death in the oppressed. This real presence should not be muted or obscured with loose language about the Eucharist. The bread is his Body because first this suffering community is his body, his vicar on earth, his priestly mediation between heaven and the earth.[11]

Liberation theology usually arises from the experiences of women and men living in countries with a history of colonisation – of injustice and oppression. In Latin America, Asia, Africa and the minority communities of American Indians, Blacks and Hispanics in the USA, churches are discovering inspiration in the figure of Christ as the poor one who is with them in their suffering and their struggle. While there are differences of emphasis among those who would gather under the banner of liberation theology, there are enough convergences to describe it as a formidable movement which is energising and renewing the churches in those countries – though not, of course, without tension, pain and struggle.

This movement reflects the struggle of Christians engaged in a revolutionary movement to extricate themselves from the slavery of colonial capitalism which upholds order and property, but always at the expense of the poor. It also shows that a vision of the future is not the sole prerogative of Marxists. Such Christians experience the Gospel, the good news, as news which liberates them, and potentially all. They experience the good news of the coming of the kingdom in their struggle for justice, where their sense of shame and humiliation is cast off and their dignity as women and men formed in God's image is affirmed.

They have also brought to the Church a way of understand-

ing theology which nourishes and strengthens them individ-
ually and together as Christian communities. It is a theology
which is no longer studied by academics in universities or institutions. Now it is alive in communities, in townships, in vil-
lages, in slums – wherever people gather together to tell their
stories, often with much pain, in the light of the story of Jesus as
they see him in the Gospels. Theology is no longer the applica-
tion of timeless generalised truth, but a living process of reflecting and making connections between one's own experience,
the insights and stories of the Bible, and the experiences of the
Christian tradition over nearly 2000 years.

There is nothing deadly about liberation theology. But there
is both terrible agony and amazing hope. Liberation theology
goes with martyrdom – in Central and South America, South
Africa as well as South Korea, Singapore, Malaysia and the Philippines. Thousands of laypeople, nuns and monks, priests and
bishops have disappeared, been exiled, tortured or murdered
for standing with God on the side of the oppressed. And yet
from their suffering there are many, known and unknown, who
in the quality of their lives display a courage and radiance
which is transparent with the love of God. I am thinking of
Oscar Romero of El Salvador and his martyrdom in 1979, of the
heroic poverty of Bishop Pedro Casaldaliga in Brazil, of the
courage of Archbishop Desmond Tutu in South Africa, and of
the Christians in the Philippines. These individuals have to
become our teachers, our evangelists. They are the missionaries
of our time.

The quality of Third World Christian communities – many
of them poor, frail and needy – is an example to the declining
and dying churches of the First World. In Asia, people are
learning how to be Christian in countries with a non-Christian
majority composed of other religions. In Latin America, Christians are showing how to take the side of the poor in their
struggle for liberation. In Africa, Christians are taking ancient
non-Christian cultures into account in their liturgies in order to
redesign and rediscover Christian celebration.

Could such a Jesus Christ – the saviour and liberator of the

poor – become ours in Europe? At St James's Church, Piccadilly, I have welcomed many from the Third World – from El
Salvador, Soweto in South Africa, from Chile, Nicaragua and
the Philippines. It has always been a privilege to receive the
witnesses of these frequently poor, frail, struggling Christian
communities because they are invariably people of great hope
and vitality. Many have suffered but their hope is indomitable.
They and their churches could be described as examples to us
in Europe. But that is not so. We have to find our own way.

I believe the recovery of Jesus Christ as the one who is first of
all good news for the poor, and invites them into his kingdom
before all others, is one of the fundamental insights of our time,
which shines through all the ambiguities and questions about
the Jesus of history. The Gospels are for the poor first: that is,
for us in the United Kingdom, for single parents, the long-term
unemployed, the alienated young black women and men, the
elderly. Such people, and all living in our urban priority areas,
have to define who Christ is for them.

And that is the difficulty. Most Third World liberation theology emerges either in rural communities or at least in
communities which have not experienced the industrial and
technological revolutions. In Latin America or Central America, the homes of liberation theology, there is a strong Christian
Catholic culture which prevails. It works. It can be recon-
structed and reinterpreted. Such communities have not experienced the gradual secularisation of society as European urban
society has, where Christian symbols and Christian mythology
are often almost unknown.

In Europe, city life for the poor offers nothing certain beyond
itself. It is a self-contained, self-sufficient experience. There is
little sense of anything beyond survival, no awareness that the
enormously complex life of the city is itself dependent for its
very existence on God's Creation. For many generations we
have been taught that the only certainties lie in what can be
tested and proved and seen, and all the rest is wishful thinking.
It is this mind set which prevents the presence and power of
God from breaking in and offering newness and vitality. It is

this which makes the naming of Christ so problematic, so difficult.

At the end of *Mersey Reflections on Faith in the City*, the group
who had been reflecting on faith in Merseyside came to this
conclusion:

> Perhaps the crucial and painful point is to recognise the need to
> live with these questions, to recognise that the apparent death
> of God is a desert experience, a time for alert waiting, for being pre-
> sent for and with people. A time for prophetic imagination, for
> naming and unmasking the powers that dominate people's lives,
> for living out alternatives, subversive, non-conformist, creative
> alternatives. A time to live by promise, not by proof. A time for a
> determined process of action, reflection, prayer. A time when the
> God who comes is rediscovered within that process itself. Paths are
> made by those who walk them.

Nevertheless, it is possible to sketch what would happen if
the churches of the generally rich and privileged (certainly all
of us compared to most Third World churches) were to see
through the eyes of the poor, and discern their strength, resilience and courage – both nationally and globally. The mecha-
nism which produces poverty has to be understood and
brought to light, particularly the ways in which churches have
endorsed the aggression and superiority of colonial powers.

There is a need for First World Christians to consider how
much guilt they must bear for the poverty of the Third World,
and the plundering of God's people and Creation. Our liturgies
should give us an understanding of the idolatry of the marketplace and a move away from consumerism to a simpler
lifestyle. We need to become aware of the limitations of development aid, and realise that we, as First World Christians, are
ourselves oppressors. We are rich because people in the Third
World are poor. We are fat because others starve. And we
should protest against the increasing growth of the armaments
industry – which is the chief consumer of those it supposedly
protects. There are more soldiers in the world than teachers.
More money is spent on military research than research into sources of energy, medical research, agricultural and
environmental conservation put together.

There needs to be a recognition that unless the churches of the First World respond to the opportunities and challenges of the Third World churches (and, it might be said, of the churches of the poor, homeless and frail in their own countries) they forfeit the right to be part of the one universal Church. They would show themselves to be schismatic, forsaking the unity of the Church. As St Paul says in 1 Corinthians 12:26, 'And whether one member suffer, all the members suffer with it; or one member be honoured, all the members rejoice with it.'

As this solidarity with the poor begins to grow among the rich churches of the First World, then perhaps it will really be pssible to speak of Christ as the one who brings goodness to the poor. But until this is so, it is better to say nothing. It is a terrible abuse of the poor to indulge in talk about Christ the liberator, when talk is all there is. Better to say that we have no clear picture of Christ for today rather than speak easily of the good news to the poor. For unless attitudes change and repentance becomes a possibility, it is humbug.

To end this chapter with an awareness of the world's poor is a long way from Galileo's telescope, and finding our way through the confusions about the Jesus of history. But one thing is very clear – that we should not turn Jesus into an idol so that the whole might of our faith depends on that historical person (about whom there are so many unanswered questions). Such a Jesus obscures God. Neither should we be in a hurry to answer the question: Who is Christ for us today? Perhaps the Church in Europe is entering a time of uncertainty and darkness, and the most that can be done is to face up to that as bravely and as honestly as possible. After all, everything that grows needs a time of darkness before birth.

6

GUILT, SIN, SALVATION AND ATONEMENT

There is a crisis about religious language. Sometimes the meaning of religious words is not at all clear. And this applies to the four words to be considered in this chapter. The first one is 'guilt'. Someone who is guilty may be nervous or anxious. Anxiety is recognisable, but the closer we get to guilt the more difficult it is to define. Then there is 'sin', which almost invariably refers to sexual misbehaviour. Any other connotations are vague. There are the seven deadly sins, of which lust is the most well known. But I suspect many people would find it difficult to name the other six, without a lot of thought.

As the words become more abstract their meanings, and the experiences they convey, slip out of reach, out of sight. An example is the word 'salvation'. There are some meagre associations with being saved. We might say, 'Marrying her was his salvation.' But in a religious context, there is often confusion. It might mean being saved from hellfire. However, it is often not clear from what, and by whom, and in what direction, salvation is being offered.

Finally there is 'atonement' – not exactly an everyday word. Atoning seems a particularly stiff way of talking about 'making up'. Many Christians would disagree with these definitions. They would say something like: God made the world. Adam and Eve were our first parents from whom we are descended.

They were given freedom to choose good or evil. They were disobedient and chose evil. They were expelled from Paradise. Their and our depravity was eased by God, who sent his Son to save us. Their and our sin had estranged us from God. Thus God the Father offers his Son as a sacrifice. He shed his blood on our behalf. Thus we are reconciled with God. The salvation thus procured (and only through the Cross of Christ) is available to those who repent, say their prayers, study the Bible as the inerrant Word of God, and live as good lives as can be expected. At death, all being well, heaven awaits those who have already repented and turned to Jesus Christ as their saviour.

For me, this story – a framework in which the concepts of guilt, sin, salvation and atonement, fit easily – is problematic, even though it is compelling and powerful. Creation is not a historical event. Adam is not a historical figure. The now generally accepted understanding of evolution points to quite another process.

One can, of course, believe in a story beginning in a paradisal state of perfect grace and union without believing literally in the account of the Creation in Genesis. That story can also acknowledge the flawed nature of humankind with all the resulting tragic possibilities we have noted without saying that Adam and Eve were our first parents. If that is a more accurate perception of the beginning, could it not also be logically true of the end – God's judgement on each of us, the final judgement, purgatory, heaven and hell?

Here the story fragments, and the Christian tradition is deeply divided. There are those, for example, who believe it is possible to forecast when judgement is coming. They may predict a period of war and strife beforehand, and say that a spell in purgatory is mandatory for everyone. Others say that ultimately everyone will be received into heaven – and therefore hell, if there is a hell, is only a temporary resting-place! Granted that there are these different schools of thought, the Jewish Christian tradition points towards an end. Does anything more need to be said?

If the beginning and end of the drama are to be perceived less literally, and more as a story which tries to make sense of reality, then what about the central figure – Jesus Christ? If the story of Creation, Fall and the end need not be tied so directly to history, then why should that not apply to Jesus Christ? Is it necessary for redemption and salvation to be linked so directly, so unshakably, to the person of Christ? Are we asking more of Christ than that figure can possibly bear? The answers to these questions are complex because they could threaten or reinforce the entire structure of belief which has sustained Christianity for 2000 years. At this point in our exploration I need to step carefully and quietly, raising the questions and leaving them there – out in the open for all to gaze at.

Without at least a secure framework in which guilt, sin, salvation and atonement can operate, it is difficult to plumb the depths of their meaning, though an attempt can be made. First, however, it has to be noted that sin has too often been trivialised and distorted. 'Living in sin' (i.e. with someone to whom one is not married) says it all in a very old-fashioned way. Here, sin is understood as turning from God to the pleasures of the world. And repentance, according to this definition, means turning away from the world. It encourages an egocentric, neurotic, barren type of asceticism.

Consciousness of sin depends on guilt. And the way that institutional religion has exploited guilt is one of its most disgraceful aspects. Harry Williams, in his essay 'Theology and Self Awareness' published in *Soundings*, has this to say about the 1662 Holy Communion Service in the Prayer Book:

> The God, for instance, of the Book of Common Prayer seems sometimes to be a merciless egocentric tyrant, incapable of love, and thus having to be manipulated or cajoled into receiving his children. The general confession, with its repeated and elaborate protestations of guilt, looks like a desperate attempt to persuade God to accept us on the score of our eating the maximum dust possible. Even after the absolution we are uncertain whether we have succeeded in our project. We must be reassured by four quotations from Scripture. The words of our Saviour Christ are not enough. They must be reinforced by what is said by St Paul and St John.

This repeated affirmation of what is claimed as a certain fact indicates, and must often produce, doubt of its truth. One would not, for instance, in an airliner feel very comfortable if an announcement that all was well was made twice by the pilot, then by the wireless operator, then by the stewardess. One might be excused for fearing that something was seriously wrong. It is inevitable that what looks like Cranmer's deep lack of faith in God's mercy should communicate itself to many who use his liturgy, and should produce in them that spirit of bondage again unto fear from which Christ came to deliver us. This is all the more likely with the Prayer of Humble Access coming between the Sanctus and the Consecration Prayer. Unless, to the very last, we assure God of our unworthiness so much as to gather up the crumbs under his table, he may lock the dining room door in our face.[1]

But the most blatant example of evoking guilt that I am aware of is in the most solemn part of the Catholic liturgy for Good Friday – the Veneration of the Cross. Jacques Pohier describes this vividly:

Two officiants held the cross in their hand and presented it to us, singing a long entreaty placed in the mouth of God and punctuated by a refrain, 'O my people, what have I done? How have I grieved you? Tell me.' The couplets which came between the refrain made God enumerate one or other of the benefits which he had heaped on his people (that is to say, all of us, not just the Jews), and each time the reminder was followed by the description of ill-treatment or insults which human beings had inflicted on Jesus of Nazareth: 'For love of you, I smote the Egyptians . . . and you scourged me before delivering me up . . . I opened the waters of the river before you. And with a spear-thrust you opened my heart. I gave you living water which sprang from the rock, and you gave me gall and vinegar to drink . . . I raised you above the others by my omnipotence; and you raised me up on the tree of the cross.' 'O my people, what have I done for you . . .' O my people, dozens of times; it was the best part of the office not only musically but also dramatically. Dozens of times I prayed this dialogue in which everything possible was done to evoke both compassion towards Christ and consternation at the way in which we treated him through our lives as a result of our sin.[2]

Jacques Pohier makes the simple point that in the narrative of the Passion read during the Good Friday liturgy, Jesus is mostly silent. He never complains. He never says, 'O my people, what have I done for you?' He never produces a list of all the good things he has done to overwhelm us with shame by making us produce a list of our sins. Nowhere in the Gospels does he say, 'Why have you done that to me after all I've done for you?' 'Aren't you ashamed?' Jesus suffers but he never moans. He never complains. He does not say, 'What do you think you are doing?' 'How could you have done that to me after all I've done for you?' 'I must be fond of you to forgive you after all you are doing to me.'

Rather, as Jacques Pohier says:

> When Jesus takes the initiative in the encounter, or in the majority of the encounters in which his various conversation partners take the initiative, he never asks the other person to recognise that he or she is a sinner so that they may claim the right to speak with him, to become the object of his attention. Jesus never presents himself as occupying a position which he only holds to the degree that people confess their sin to him and ask for forgiveness. So, to take up the words of the Miserere again, this is not the way in which he proved to be right, nor is it the attitude that he wanted to have towards human beings. He had other and better things to do; he had other and better things to bring out in others; he was in more of a hurry: 'Zaccaeus, I want to eat with you this evening.'[3]

The original acceptance and unconditional concern for those whom Jesus ate with gave way to an expression of the gulf between God and ourselves, and of our own appalling unworthiness and badness. Jesus – the paradigm and founder of Christianity – was displaced, removed and the God of institutional religion replaced him.

It is easy to see why. It is after all in the interest of order and some sort of peace that the powerful – the clergy – need to remind people how worthless they are, and how through the clergy, and them alone, God's mercy is mediated. In order to win the approval and love of God, Christians seem to need to show him how guilty, worthless and bad they are. This is one of the mechanisms by which guilt is nourished in Christianity. It is also why people leave their churches; they sense the disease of institutions which foster such attitudes. Years ago a social worker told me, 'I spend my time trying to hold people together: you clergy undermine all we do by saying how worthless people are.' I am not denying guilt and sin but I am trying to point out some of the neurotic tendencies which religious people easily fall prey to.

Guilt is a complex phenomenon. It is easily confused with shame. Many of the actions we think of as sinful are more to do with shame, and what people think of us. An incident from my own life, not so uncommon, makes the point. After my mother died, my father lived on his own at home. As he grew older, I tried to arrange all sorts of systems of support which would enable him to stay at home. It was clear that this was what he wanted to do.

During this time I was badgered by my relatives to get him into an old people's home where he could be looked after properly; they certainly had a point, because they were part of the support system. When it was clear that he could stay at home no longer, questions arose as to where he should go. Should he live with me? That would be sensible – but a rectory in central London was hardly the place for a man in his mid-eighties. So he went to the old people's home.

Once he was there, I felt much unspoken criticism for not visiting him enough and taking care of him. There were complaints of negligence from my family, 'and you a priest', they would say. As far as I could tell, my father was happy in the home, and my rather desultory relationship with him flowered a little.

During this time, I was not sure whether I had done the right thing or not. I felt ashamed and guilty that I did not visit him as much as everyone else. On the other hand, given the distance involved, I was not sure what more I could have done. Where was the shame? Was it in trying to placate my relations? And where was the guilt, if guilt there was? At the time it was confusing, and only after his death did I feel that I really had done the best I could. Not until then did I realise that my guilt had got mixed up with my shame at what other people were thinking.

Furthermore, guilt is easily misplaced. Because Christianity has dwelt on guilt and alienation from God, Christians have been urged to be humble and passive. Insubordination is not usually considered a Christian virtue – obedience is expected. But sometimes consciences are awakened, and it becomes impossible to remain silent. Totalitarian regimes mobilise their military and security forces to destroy dissenters. In our own society many of these dissenters are marginalised and ridiculed because they dare to comment, doubt and question.

I experienced this sharply in 1982 when I belonged to a small group who opposed the way in which the British government responded to the Argentinian invasion of the Falkland Islands. We made our protest known and I received letters, and much verbal abuse, accusing me of being unpatriotic and a traitor. I began to wonder whether that was indeed so, and even to feel guilty about the modest stand I had taken. Guilt had begun to cloud what had originally been a clear matter of conscience.

Sin is our primary concern. Sin is a religious word which has a wealth of meaning far beyond sexual misbehaviour or a vague sense of wrong-doing. Wherever sin occurs, God is hurt and offended. To sin is to sin against God and against everything that is good. But sin is not just an action against God and God's goodness, it is also the failure to do good. This is summed up in a letter from the film director Pasolini to the Pope, 'Sin does not mean doing wrong; not to do good – that's what sin means.'

Once these confusions about guilt have been exposed, it should not be necessary to say much more about guilt. Sin is not measured by the suffering it causes the sinner! Trivial sins are often enlarged out of all proportion because of intense awareness of guilt, when the suffering involved is comparatively small. But once guilt is present in any situation, even a hint of it, that is enough. It should be 'confessed', forgotten, and steps taken to see that occasions for it do not arise again.

Sin means not appreciating and enjoying the wonders of Creation in the sense that children do (although of course they are not sinless). It means refusing to be responsible for one another, and the sustaining of Creation; it means ignoring the injuries we inflict on the planet and refusing to accept the diversity of Creation – the rich tapestry of peoples and every sort of life of which we are a part. Sin is defining everyone else in the light of our own prejudices, and not allowing the differences of others to flourish, be enjoyed and celebrated. To refuse to encourage all the possibilities offered by a multi-racial world is sinful; to refuse to recognise the contributions that lesbian and gay people, gypsies, and any other minority might make, is sinful.

Sin is awesome in its varied manifestations – not least when we consider it in relation to God who, as I have tried to show, is infinitely and intimately involved with the world; God flinches at the tiniest creature's suffering.

Blindness and indifference to pain and injustice are also a form of sin. The sinner does not see, for example, that by doing nothing, he or she is colluding with an economic system which allows millions in the Third World to die of starvation. When many die at the hands of torturers and secret police, and these cruelties are known but ignored, then such silence is sinful. Not to notice what is happening is blindness, and it is sinful.

Sin is going it alone and to hell with what anyone else thinks; it is a refusal to recognise our interdependence. Sin is always committed by individuals. But any sin affects others; it can become embodied in the way communities function. It is in this sense that we can speak of social or structural sin. A whole society can thus be infected, so that it is possible to speak of that society as being evil – either in part or as a whole. For example, in the United Kingdom, the laws about immigration reflect the racism of individuals but the infection spreads to the way we treat entire communities. That is social sin.

And then the prospect of sinning is attractive. Like evil, as we have seen, it presents an attractive façade. It offers the prospect that we can be like God. Nowhere is this more apparent than in the use of nuclear power. We have the ability to destroy Creation within minutes – that is, to uncreate the world of God. So someone, somewhere, has their finger on the button:

> Let us try to be God, let us destroy the world, just to see what it is like. Never mind that we shall destroy ourselves in the process. There is, after all, not much point in living – and one more new experience is worth having, isn't it? Let's just see. Come on, are you ready? For a moment we will hold the Earth in our hands before we blow ourselves and our future out of existence!

That is madness. That is sin – in its most final and desperate manifestation. It's the ultimate abdication of responsibility for doing good. And in such a situation – new in the history of civilisation – we are all victims and perpetrators alike. It is this which gives sin a tragic dimension.

Aware of the many dimensions of sin, and the suffering it has caused, apathy seems to be the usual response. 'What can I do?' 'Nothing' is the answer, so the sin is compounded. It seems that desire for unity and communion with one another and with what we know of God is thwarted in every way. But that is not so, for Christianity has always taught that the answer to sin and evil is salvation. As long as that sentence has been allowed to remain abstract, Christians have been happy to agree that it is so. But as soon as it is interpreted and examined in detail, there are many disagreements.

Salvation, it is said, comes through Jesus Christ our Lord and Saviour. The classic view – in keeping with the outmoded mythology I have already described – is that Jesus acts alone. Through his death on the cross, he took away the sins of the world; the Agnus Dei in the Eucharist says: 'O Lamb of God that takest away the sins of the world, have mercy upon us.'

The meaning of his death has been interpreted in many ways. It was a victory over the devil, and 2000 years later the mopping-up operation is still going on. It was a ransom paid to the devil. It was a sacrifice to placate an angry God who could then show his mercy. In whatever way his death is understood, it offers some sort of salvation, and creates the conditions for reconciliation between God and humankind. The benefits of this reconciliation are received through preaching and the sacraments. The forgiveness of sins is announced and celebrated.

I find many difficulties with these classic formulations. It makes no sense to me that in some incoherent way we share in this atoning, reconciling death 2000 years later. That sort of solidarity is difficult to believe in. And I have already touched on other problems: the lack of precise information about Jesus and how he perceived his mission; as well as the question of Jesus representing the whole human race (black people and women, as we saw, find this particularly difficult to accept). And if Jesus is not a representative person, then it is hard to see how his death has affected the whole course of human history.

The traditional formulations are addressed to individuals; forgiveness is offered to each human soul on its ascent to God with the promise of life after death. But if salvation is confined to this individual spiritual realm, what about the saving of a world which is broken, shattered and crying for justice and healing? This is where salvation has to find a home, not just in the soul of the individual. And this means that we do not sit passively and accept the salvation offered to us, but that we, together with God, perform salvation. God needs us. There is no one else available to perform the works of salvation.

Like a lover, God invites a response from us – God's beloved – and that response is the work of salvation in whatever form it takes. For some it is the pursuit of justice. For others it is searching for reconciliation. For some it is the healing of bodies as well as souls. For some it is resisting oppression and injustice. For others it is allaying the pain of the Earth. And the work of salvation is always reaching out; it has a beautiful, radical and inclusive quality about it.

Salvation happens when the individual turns from preoccupation with self to a concern and passion for the well-being of the world. Sallie McFague lists some of her saviours – women and men who revealed the 'passionate, valuing, inclusive love for the world that we see in the figure of Jesus'.[4] They include: John Woolman, the eighteenth-century Quaker abolitionist; Dietrich Bonhoeffer; Dorothy Day; Mahatma Gandhi; and an amazing American woman, Sojourner Truth, 'an illiterate slave and mother of twelve children, all but one sold away from her. She was emancipated in 1827 to begin an itinerant ministry after a religious experience in which she responded, "Oh God, I did not know you were so big": a ministry of abolitionism and women's rights, the overcoming of the divisions of slave and slaveholder, women and men.'[5]

It is in the lives of such people, known and unknown, that salvation is happening today. It is as if they love the world with such passion and in such radical and inclusive ways that they reflect another picture of God as lover. God as lover of Creation says that the beloved is of infinite value and infinitely precious. Love knows no limits. And the lover's heart is broken when those who are valued are hurt, humiliated, bruised and rejected – because he sees himself in their broken bodies and pained faces. God is sinned against in the faces of all victims and in the scarred Earth.

Perhaps the idea that God is among the victims helps to illuminate the death of Jesus. If God is 'like Jesus' and if Jesus is a window into God, then what does the cross convey? In the Roman Empire, the cross was the means by which murderers and criminals were publicly executed. Jesus was nailed to such a cross. He was a victim, an innocent victim, and the whole drift and movement of the Christian tradition – when it is most faithful to its origins, despite all the difficulties, confusions and ambiguities – is not the Jesus who absolved our sins 2000 years ago, and who now reigns in heaven triumphant, but Jesus the victim, the crucified and suffering God.

In our own day, there are many who bear the sins of our society; they are especially the poor who reproach the rest of us. Their eyes are the eyes of God. They are as good or bad as anyone. That is not the point. That they have no voice, no choice and no power is not of their own doing. There is a profound innocence about the situation of the poor; and that is how they reflect the image of God. To become aware of this astonishing insight is shattering and breathtaking. It encourages, confirms and strengthens resolve, for the poor reveal to us our idols and idolatries, the fragile nature of our security, and our dependence on one another. They become our teachers and they show us, in their collective innocence, the way to salvation.

I would like to end these reflections by acknowledging the difficulty of writing about these profound matters. We are living, in terms of our Christian faith, in a wilderness. A lot of what is said about God is meaningless, especially when the comments are about those who unwittingly show God – the poor. Dietrich Bonhoeffer said it all forty years ago, in a letter to his friend Eberhard Bethge:

> We are once again being driven right back to the beginnings of our understanding. Reconciliation and redemption, regeneration and the Holy Spirit, love of our enemies, cross and resurrection, life in Christ and Christian discipleship – all these are so difficult and so remote that we hardly venture any more to speak of them. In the traditional words and acts we suspect there may be something quite new and revolutionary, though we cannot as yet grasp or express it. . . . Our Church, which has been fighting . . . only for its self-preservation, as though that were an end in itself, is incapable of taking the word of reconciliation and redemption to mankind and the world. Our earlier words are therefore bound to lose their force and cease, and our being Christian today will be limited to two things: prayer and righteous action among men. All Christian thinking, speaking, and organising must be born anew out of this prayer and action. . . . Any attempt to help the Church prematurely to a new expansion of its organisation will merely delay its conversion and purification.'[6]

A sign of this desert experience is the lack of hope. One of the characteristics of salvation, and that which distinguishes it from ideologies of one sort or another, is hope. (The cross always has to be seen in the context of the resurrection.) Hope makes us aware of the challenges which have to be taken up (say in social or political activity), and the sense of challenge is sustained by hope, particularly as this is generated in shared life and communal celebration. The hope which springs from this type of 'saving' work is always reaching out, broadening its concern so that it might encompass the whole.

Hope is not a quality we experience much in our own country, among the rich or the poor. Yet I have always been struck by the resilence, courage and hope of people from Soweto or the Philippines, El Salvador or Nicaragua. Many of these people have suffered imprisonment, are regularly harassed by the police and are often in danger of their lives.

Such hope is missing in our country. Our advanced, but decaying, industrial society seems to have dulled our imaginations, so that we cannot envision a life any different from what we know. And this is particularly true of the victims or casualties of the marketplace: the poor, the needy and the unemployed. The difficulties of speaking about these issues of sin and salvation are increased by the fact that nowadays talk of God is generally regarded as a matter of private opinion, wishful thinking or fantasy.

There are no easy solutions. There is the call to face up to what is happening and who does what to whom, and why. There is the need to unmask the idolatries. And all this has to be undertaken from the perspective of the poor, for that is the perspective of the Bible and of Jesus. Maybe then a sense of sin will emerge, and the struggle for salvation begin. The symbols and stories of Christianity support, encourage and nourish such analysis. And then comes the working out of salvation together with, and in the company of God who, as a friend, has promised always to be with us.

7

EVIL AND SUFFERING

I would hesitate to describe a person as evil. Mean, selfish, bigoted, cruel maybe, but evil – that is another matter. To call a person evil is to imply that he or she is beyond redemption; there is no hope for them. Moreover, we have been persuaded by the media that evil people are particularly unusual – murderers, for example, like Myra Hindley, Ian Brady, Peter Sutcliffe, Dennis Nilsen or Jeremy Bamber. They are not like us.

Yet my experience is rather different. Evil is a pervasive and mysterious phenomenon which is found in individuals, in families and in societies. The universe itself seems to be fatally flawed and twisted; a dark and tragic place.

The Nature of Evil

Evil is difficult to describe. It is a mystery which cannot be explained, but it can be approached. Evil people are those who kill. They are murderers. They are those who seek to destroy the human spirit. They are against life in all its forms. When the writer and philosopher Hannah Arendt spoke about 'the banality of evil',[1] she did not mean to trivialise it, but to draw our attention to the dreariness and drabness of those who are evil. Evil people are not always criminals; neither do they have devil's horns, forked tongues and all the other paraphernalia of devil mythology.

Children and young people are often the victims of evil. Michael, a young man in his early twenties, came to see me. He told me he was always thinking of death. When he went to a family funeral he resented the fact that he was not lying in the coffin instead of his elderly uncle. His depression was easily recognisable – he could not establish any intimate relationships, and he was unwilling to express or share his feelings.

After a few meetings he began to talk about his childhood. His parents were respectable, hard-working, lower middle-class people, and Michael was their only child. He told me how his parents had emotionally abandoned him when he was born; they had wanted a girl, and instead they got Michael. Throughout his childhood he had been victimised, beaten and ignored. He was not wanted. He had been, as he told me, 'a mistake'. And he wanted to die.

His parents, I learnt, were active members of their church and of other local organisations. Michael told me they used to have lots of meetings in the front room where people would study the Bible together. He was told to go to his room when these gatherings took place. He hated the Bible. During his adolescence he had a lot of trouble at school; he was caught stealing, and was accused of being disruptive. His parents became more and more exasperated with him. The more delinquent his behaviour became, the more they threatened him.

When I met Michael, he felt he was completely unlovable, worthless and bad. He was convinced that he was rotten to the core. I never met his parents, but as our conversations developed I came to see that they were evil. For reasons I could not fathom, they wished to destroy their son. Their lives were a cover-up. They concealed their evil, seeing themselves as faultless. They were dedicated to keeping up their appearance of respectability and their arrogance was truly astonishing. They believed they were beyond any sort of reproach. Whenever Michael queried something they said, they would lash out at him – projecting their own evil on their son. The parents denied their own badness, and were absorbed in their conviction that they were perfect.

As far as I could tell they worked together, mutually supporting one another in destroying their son. This form of child abuse is far more rampant and quite as disturbing as sexual child abuse. What made Michael's parents evil was the consistency of their behaviour. Many criminal acts are committed by accident. But, listening to Michael's story, it was clear that the parents had unconsciously created a pact with one another to destroy their son's spirit. No psychological categories I know are adequate to describe their condition except that of evil.

They were the ones who should have come to our counselling sessions. But counselling of any kind is intrusive. They would have shunned the light, the necessary scrutiny, which exposed their lives as evil. As far as I know, they are still prominent members of their church. Their public persona remains untarnished.

Michael had a severe breakdown, but as I write is slowly beginning to recover, discovering that he is worthwhile and starting to form relationships. He no longer sees his parents.

I am not a therapist, so I cannot produce clinical evidence about the extent of this evil, but my observation is that Michael is not an unusual example of someone who has experienced the impact of evil parents; it is part of the human condition. Evil may be going on in your neighbours' homes, however respectable they appear to be.

But individuals are not isolated examples of evil. It can be encountered in groups, communities and nations. Millions of people, knowingly or unknowingly, contributed to the Nazi Holocaust; many participated in the slaughter of innocent people in Amin's Uganda and Pol Pot's Cambodia. The roots of this kind of collective evil become so deeply embedded in a political or social system that everything about that system becomes corrupt. Albert Nolan, writing in *God in South Africa*, says:

It would be impossible to exaggerate the evil of the system in South Africa. It has wrought havoc in the lives of people, caused a barbarous excess of violence and suffering, deprived people of their humanity, produced blindness, alienation and violent conflict. All that it can promise us is that the poor will become poorer and the blind blinder, that there will be more conflict, more bloodshed and total chaos. . . . Our struggle is not against flesh and blood, but against the evil spirit that is embodied in the system.[2]

Why do we participate in evil? How is it that perfectly 'normal' ordinary people can together perpetrate the most appalling acts which contradict all notions of what it means to be human? One of the best-documented cases of such collective evil occurred in March 1968 when a US Army platoon went in search of Viet Cong soldiers. They arrived at the village of My Lai in South Vietnam. No Viet Cong were found. But some 500 unarmed civilians were shot – some where they stood, others rounded up in front of a ditch and then shot. Women were raped before being killed. Old men and children were among the victims. When it was all over, the soldiers sat down and rested among the bodies and had lunch.

This incident has been well documented and interpreted, although initially attempts were made to cover it up. What emerges from the accounts of those who were there, and those who arrived shortly after the massacre, was that the soldiers had been so thoroughly brainwashed that they did not know what they were doing. The enemy had become objects; they had been dehumanised. They were not men, women or children – just 'dinks' or 'gooks'.

The soldiers were only doing what they were told: giving orders; obeying orders. Orders first; questions afterwards. Their training had been so thorough that nothing could have prevented these atrocities. And the US Army is a mammoth, complex organisation where no one is completely responsible, all are partly responsible and it is impossible to pin responsibility to one person. Thus, institutions breed and compound evil.

But what the My Lai massacre really showed was the capacity of ordinary, decent, normal human beings, when all restraints are removed, to be destructive just for the pleasure of it. At My

Lai the soldiers were free to unleash the darkest and cruellest aspects of their personalities.

Evil does not only exist in individuals, groups and communities. There is also the evil inherent in Nature, and the way in which we misuse Creation. To work properly, any ecological system depends on delicate balances which ensure the continuity of life. Inevitably, in this larger scale of things, individuals and species are sacrificed for the continuing life of the whole. I am not saying that natural selection, or the process of evolution itself is evil – only that, as many television documentaries show, Nature is 'red in tooth and claw'. A measure of evil, or at least cruelty, is built into the way Nature functions.

Furthermore, however concerned we may be about the state of the planet, it seems we just do not want to do anything about it. Thus the rainforests which are absolutely essential to the continuation of life, providing oxygen and water, are endangered because of the rapid increase of the human population. Of course, we need to know how to tackle these complex and urgent problems, but knowledge is not the primary consideration. (Sooner or later solutions might be found.) The issue is one of will.

One of the strengths of the Christian tradition is that it is so aware of the power and presence of evil, the sin which gives rise to it, and the suffering which follows from it. Evil reveals a tragic dimension to existence; it cannot be explained away. The depths of this tragedy have been conveyed in many different ways. Shakespeare's tragedies have a cosmic dimension. In *Macbeth*, for example, the King, who is the anointed one and the highest in the hierarchy of beings, is murdered. All hell is let loose. The cosmic order is disrupted and life is turned upside-down:

ROSS   Ah, good father,
    Thou seest, the heavens, as troubled with man's act,
    Threatens the bloody stage. By th' clock 'tis day,
    And yet dark night strangles the travelling lamp.

> Is't night's predominance, or the day's shame,
> That darkness does the face of earth entomb,
> When living light should kiss it?
>
> OLD MAN   'Tis unnatural,
> Even like the deed that's done. On Tuesday last,
> A falcon, tow'ring in her pride of place,
> Was by a mousing owl hawk'd at and kill'd.
>
> ROSS And Duncan's horses – a thing most strange and certain –
> Beauteous and swift, the minions of their race,
> Turn'd wild in nature, broke their stalls, flung out,
> Contending 'gainst obedience, as they would make
> War with mankind.
>
> OLD MAN   'Tis said they eat each other.[3]

The Renaissance idea expressed here of the great chain of being belongs to a bygone age, but the universal disturbance unleashed by the eruption of evil is still powerfully conveyed in horror films, for example, by sudden winds, thunder and lightning, leaves swirling around and the appearance of monsters and devils. All these herald the release of forces beyond our control, beyond all reason. Nature runs riot.

The unbridled energy of Nature holds us in awe. In the same way we are entranced by the power displayed by murderers in dominating and destroying their victims. When Ian Brady and Myra Hindley murdered their young victims, the natural order was disrupted. As I have suggested, evil actions find echoes deep within ourselves. We become aware of feelings and violent emotions which we normally ignore and which society, rightly, inhibits. I can remember, for example, feeling such rage against another that I could barely contain it. That rage was directed at someone whom I both loved and hated. Murderers, child murderers and mass murderers mirror the worst side of ourselves. Why else do we go to the Chamber of Horrors?

As I have said, evil people and evil societies sometimes present themselves in a respectable guise. But equally evil will dress up as goodness, radiating attraction and some sort of beauty. In Subniv Babuta and Jean-Claude Bragard's *Evil*, the authors speak of the attraction of evil, particularly of evil as personified by Satan in Milton's *Paradise Lost*:

Satan is . . . grand, defiant, majestic, courageous, independent, a voyager into the unknown. Whereas we tend to equate evil with cruelty, Milton does not make Satan primarily cruel. He is a great leader, full of concern for his troops, his courage and strength undaunted by his misfortune.[4]

The most evocative and detailed account of evil in the Bible is found throughout the Book of Revelations. The author is not concerned with the origins of evil, but with its manifestation and ultimate exodus. He has a truly cosmic sense of evil and the corruption which affects the entire human order. He uses the symbols of the monster and the whore, one representing political tyranny, the other the economic seductions of the state. This author identifies these symbols with the Roman Empire, but both monster and whore have longer pedigrees stretching back to Babylon and the symbolic names of Sodom and Egypt. The monster and the whore delude the whole world.

The author uses the most offensive language he can find to describe his enemies, because he recognises how evil presents itself in a most attractive light. Evil in its nakedness does not last long. So Satan is the deceiver of the whole world who deliberately misleads humankind by lying about God. The monster is the AntiChrist. He is a travesty of the Lamb, bearing the marks of the crucified Christ. In Chapter 17:4 the whore is made superficially attractive: 'And the woman was arrayed in purple and scarlet colour, and decked with gold and precious stones and pearls, having a golden cup in her hand full of abominations and filthiness of her fornication.'

Chapter 18:15-19 contains some of the most vivid lamentations in literature about the destruction of a city. Here the author, through the very wistfulness of his language, shows how the seductive power of Rome nearly ensnared him:

The merchants of these things, which were made rich by her, shall stand afar off for the fear of her torment, weeping and wailing. And saying, Alas, alas that great city, that was clothed in fine linen, and purple, and scarlet, and decked with gold, and precious stones, and pearls! For in one hour so great riches is come to naught. And every shipmaster, and all the company in ships, and sailors, and as many as trade by sea, stood afar off, and cried when they saw the smoke of her burning, saying, What city is like unto this great city! And they cast dust on their heads, and cried, weeping and wailing, saying, Alas, alas that great city, wherein were made rich all that had ships in the sea by reason of her costliness, for in one hour she is made desolate.

In our own day wicked dictatorships are upheld by sophisticated propaganda machinery which presents a human and good face to the world. How many were hoodwinked by Nazism? In some cases, as in South Africa, the government claims it is Christian, presenting its policies in the name of Christ. And many are deceived.

I have tried to indicate some of the characteristics of evil. I do not believe there is a Devil, but making the Devil personal draws attention to the pervasive, persistent, powerful presence of evil. And the Devil is as vivid a way as any to express this.

Making Sense of Evil?

Of all the subjects covered in this book, the phenomenon of evil in all its manifestations is the hardest to make sense of. W. Somerset Maugham, in *The Summing Up*, put it succinctly: 'There is no explanation for evil. It must be looked upon as a necessary part of the order of the universe. To ignore it is childish, to bewail it senseless.'[5]

Nevertheless, explanations have to be attempted, for if, as a Christian, I believe in an omniscient, omnipotent God who is the epitome of all goodness, why does this good God permit evil? The philosopher David Hume put 'the problems of evil' quite directly: 'Is God willing to prevent evil, but not able? Then he is impotent. Is he able, but not willing? Then he is malevolent. Is he both able and willing? Whence then is evil?'[6]

These questions present the most immense, damaging and longest-standing threat to the claims of belief. No one has yet managed to provide convincing and coherent replies which do justice to the presence and power of evil in the world. The abstractions of philosophers and theologians as they engage

David Hume's questions inevitably reduce evil, and trivialise it as a matter of intellectual speculation.

If God is all-powerful and the ruler of the universe, as it were, then such a God is one who imposes suffering and stands with the victors and the oppressors, appearing wherever murder is committed. Such a God of power and might and glory expresses the sadism of those who invented him.

In 1945 we crossed a threshold in the history of civilisation with which we are still, and will be for many generations, coming to terms. The first stage was the public revelation of the deliberate attempt to destroy God's chosen people, the Jews, in the Holocaust. The second stage was the dropping of the atomic bomb on Hiroshima, thus proving that we now possessed the means to blow Creation to bits. Christian faith cannot be the same since the Holocaust and Hiroshima. These two events have brought about a severe crisis of belief in God. It is as if there has been an interruption in the way we speak of God.

In the vast literature which has grown up around the Holocaust the following episode is often related. It took place in Auschwitz in the summer of 1944, and it was told by S. Szmaglewska, a Polish guard, to the Nuremberg War Crimes Tribunal:

> WITNESS: . . . women carrying children were [always] sent with them to the crematorium. [Children were of no labour value so they were killed. The mothers were sent along, too, because separation might lead to panic and hysteria, which might slow up the destruction process, and this could not be afforded. It was simpler to condemn the mothers too and keep things quiet and smooth.] The children were then torn from their parents outside the crematorium and sent to the gas chambers separately. [At that point, crowding more people into the gas chambers became the most urgent consideration. Separating meant that more children could be packed in separately, or they could be thrown in over the heads of adults once the chambers were packed.] When the extermination of the Jews in the gas chambers was at its height, orders were issued that children were to be thrown straight into the crematorium furnaces, or into a pit near the crematorium, without being gassed first.
>
> SMIRNOV (Russian prosecutor): How am I to understand this? Did they throw them into the fire alive, or did they kill them first?

WITNESS: They threw them in alive. Their screams could be heard at the camp. It is difficult to say how many children were killed in this way.

SMIRNOV: Why did they do this?

WITNESS: It's very difficult to say. We don't know whether they wanted to economise on gas, or if it was because there was not enough room in the gas chambers.[7]

Irving Greenberg proposes that this episode should serve as an 'orienting event' or litmus test for post-Auschwitz theological formulation: 'No statement, theological or otherwise, should be made that would not be credible in the presence of the burning children.'[8]

No attempted justification of God on the part of human beings can aspire to meet this test; indeed, the very thought that it is possible for someone to say, with the sufferings of these children in mind, that God is justified, is a blasphemy. This episode can only prompt penitence and conversion; it cannot motivate a justification of God to man, even one which takes the form of an atonement.

However, saying that this episode cannot form the basis of such an atonement does not imply that there cannot, in principle, be an engagement of religious faith with the narratives generated by Auschwitz. Indeed, Elie Wiesel (the Nobel prize-winning human rights campaigner who was held in Buchenwald concentration camp) allows for this possibility in *The Gates of the Forest*. Gregor, whose faith had been destroyed by the Holocaust, has a passionate exchange with the Hasidic rabbi: 'Gregor was angry. "After what has happened to us, how can you believe in God?" With an understanding smile on his lips the rabbi answered, "How can you not believe in God after what has happened?" '[9]

There are two explanations of 'the problems of evil' in the Christian tradition – a tradition which seems to collapse when confronted with this episode and countless others which took place in Auschwitz, Treblinka and Dachau. The first is St Augustine's. He puts the finishing touches to a cosmic drama, which St Paul created.

According to St Augustine, God created angels to love and serve him. Out of envy some revolted against God. God made the world and created a single human pair – Adam and Eve. They were good, happy, immortal, innocent and ageless. They were free – free to choose good or evil. The leader of the rebellious angels, Satan, disguised himself as a serpent and tempted the couple to disobey God. They did. And the consequences for the human race have been devastating ever since, because as a result of our first parents falling from grace all human beings have become flawed with a natural tendency towards evil. The drama has, of course, a happy ending. God allowed evil so that ultimately, through the sacrifice of Jesus Christ, his love would be manifested triumphant.

The theologian John Hick points out a fundamental inconsistency:

> Augustine's basic motive was to take responsibility away from the creator and to lay it further on his creatures. But a contradiction lurks at the heart of the picture he offers. For if the creatures whom God made freely went wrong there must have been a flaw in their design. The creator, therefore, must bear the ultimate responsibility first. Surely if God created the entire universe and made it just as he wanted it with nothing to hinder him, God must still have the final responsibility for it.[10]

I do not want to believe in a God whose goodness remains intact when hearing the screams of burning children. I find it difficult to believe in a God who gives Creation total freedom. It might ease God's position, but God still has to accept responsibility for creating a world with so much freedom that the Holocaust was made possible.

The other traditions justifying the ways of God to humankind do not offer any illumination either. Augustine saw the root of the problem in the past (in the Garden of Eden), but St Irenaeus (who lived 200 years before Augustine) saw the solution in the future.

Like Augustine, his story began in the Garden of Eden when Adam and Eve were young innocents. They were expelled from Paradise because they were young and immature; they needed to grow in maturity, and so, in a sense, to God. They were pushed out of the womb of Paradise to enter a world where they, and thus the rest of humanity, had the chance to grow in life and maturity, the search for perfection continuing beyond death to heaven itself.

From Irenaeus's perspective, the world is rather like a Victorian reformatory where the experiences of suffering and hardship are opportunities for growth in the journey to perfection. Even if the suffering is too much for us on Earth, all will be well beyond the gates of death. But I cannot believe in the Irenaean God who has placed us in a world where there are so many obstacles to human fulfilment. The price is too high.

In fairness to Augustine and Irenaeus (and their various followers), it is quite wrong to treat these, or any other theologians for that matter, as if they were our contemporaries. Augustine wrote for his own time, for a Church that was settled and beginning to establish itself as the religion of the Roman Empire. He wrote about the individual soul's ascent to heaven. He believed in the necessity of conversion, and the desire for illumination from God as the means by which evil could be overcome and destroyed. In his writings there is little sense of the breadth and scope of evil in its public and private manifestations that I have tried to indicate.

What is there, then, that can be said or done? The burning of children evokes horror, silence, penitence and lastly, action – action that will stop such terrible things from ever happening again. The action is possible because amongst the countless episodes of such wickedness there are others which speak of astonishing faith, resilience and courage to affirm human dignity. The telling of such tales may begin to create a solidarity with those and all victims (and in the case of the Holocaust, the slaughtered gypsies and homosexuals, as well as the Jews) who have been abandoned by God and the world, and who know what it is to be quite alone.

But there is yet more to say. The burden of this book is that we need to discover new ways to speak of God in relation to the world, ways which will seize the imagination and the heart. We are being led to a sense of the intimacy God has with the Creation, of the closeness of a God sustaining, nurturing and caring for the planet. How, then, can such an intimate God be part of our responsibility for evil and suffering?

I have to be careful in writing about suffering. I have had some experience of failure, loss and bereavement, of jealousy and unrequited love. But that is all, apart from the everyday discomforts like the occasional headache or toothache. I have managed to avoid the pain of addictions and obsessions, such as alcoholism and anorexia, with which our atheistic and materialistic culture is so replete. I am not a workaholic, shopaholic or drug addict. I have been fortunate enough not to experience the pain of innocent suffering. I have no direct experience of some of the barbarisms in the world today: the indignity suffered by the homeless and unemployed; the humiliation of the oppressed in South Africa and parts of the Third World. All these aspects of suffering, and many others, I know only second-hand.

Because the world now sees so much suffering on an unprecedented scale – and suffering which extends well beyond what human beings do to each other, to the pain of the Earth itself – it is easy to bypass it with an excuse: 'Not all blacks suffer like this; whites also suffer; there are poor people in other countries too; it is not done deliberately; people are trying to do something about it. It is not my fault.'[11]

It is not only easy to bypass it, but also to hide it, stop it and remove it as rapidly and painlessly as possible. A society enslaved by technology and the idolatry of money inevitably perceives men and women as machines. They function; they produce; they break down. The pills and sedatives are on hand to get the person functioning and producing again as soon as possible.

But since 1945, and more fitfully before then, theologians have come to speak of a God who suffers with the Creation. Geoffrey Studdert Kennedy, known as Woodbine Willie, was an army chaplain in the First World War. His experiences made him reject the stained-glass window picture of God: 'God, I hate this splendid vision – all its splendour is a lie. God, the God I love and worship, reigns in sorrow on the tree, broken, bleeding but unconquered, very God of God to me.' All real progress, he says, is caused by the working of the suffering love in the world.

What is this suffering love? Canon W. H. Vanstone addresses this question in *Love's Endeavour, Love's Expense*. He examines the nature of authentic love and how it reflects the divine love. The love of God is limitless; there is no limit to God's creativity; God has spent and continues to spend himself in renewing Creation, in being the grace which makes the world go round. And this love is inevitably precarious. Nothing is pre-determined like 'the unwinding and display of film already made'.[12] As the movement of control is lost, something evil replaces that love. Something has gone very wrong but, and this point needs to made again and again, every act of evil yet con-tains the possibility of redemption and renewal. And the issue of God's self-giving love in Creation depends on our response as to whether it will be triumph or tragedy.

Love is vulnerable. Because God's only power is this self-giving love which, although limitless, is precarious, nothing can prevent the horrors of history, whether caused by natural disas-ter or human cruelty. This power of God in the pain of our experience seeks to redeem and restore. And here we come to the heart of the mystery of suffering. From what I have experi-enced I am able to say there is no situation which is utterly and irrevocably hopeless. Perhaps it is in this sense that I can affirm God is Almighty. And this is no abstraction.

The victims at Auschwitz, as we have seen, come to represent all humankind and affirm the dignity of the human spirit. The humiliated and oppressed, in their struggle for freedom in South Africa, manifest faith and hope for life. There are homo-sexuals who continue to care for one another, and nurture those of their number who are dying of Aids. They appreciate and enjoy life in all its fragility and promise in a way which the healthy among us can only envy. It is the testimonies of all these victims – the oppressed, the marginalised, in every country – which affirm that an inner strength is available to us all to regain possession of our essential humanity.

When I listen to the stories of those who have been turned into victims, it is possible to catch glimpses of the grace of God. In their struggles and their pain, I know that God is close; God is always there, in weakness and in strength, in pain and in sorrow, in darkness and in light. This knowledge provokes the imagination, agitates the heart and summons up anger and grief at our cruelty and wickedness. It is not knowledge of an academic or intellectual kind and it reflects the suffering and the pain of God. God suffers with the victims; Christ became a victim on the cross – suffering with all those who have been sinned against.

This weakness, this pain – words are inadequate – can yet be a source of strength; it's like a movement from death to birth, to a new life of hope. The most significant image the Bible uses for this is the experience of women, the image of giving birth. In Isaiah 42:14 and 16 the Prophet says:

> I have long time holden my peace; I have been still, and refrained myself: now will I cry like a travailing woman; I will destroy and devour at once. . . . And I will bring the blind by ways that they know not; I will lead them in paths that they have not known: I will make darkness light before them, and crooked things straight. These things I will do unto them, and not forsake them.

And St John the Evangelist says in John 16:20 and 22:

> Verily, verily, I say unto you. That ye shall weep and lament, but the world shall rejoice: and ye shall be sorrowful, but your sorrow shall be turned into joy. . . . And ye now therefore have sorrow: but I will see you again and your heart shall rejoice, and your joy no man taketh from you.

Of the experience of birth, the German theologian Dorothy Sölle writes:

> To experience such pain is actually close to the overpowering inner experience of birth. To bring a child 'into the world', to give birth, is a primitive experience in which we come very close to the secret of life. It is an experience which we undergo and bring about, in which we participate both actively and passively. It is an experience which

challenges the body, spirit and soul and causes deep changes. It is one of the great experiences of creation in which we participate. It is a mystical experience because in this regard we stand before the secret of life itself. Religions call this secret life 'God', and my religious tradition includes the pain in the secret of life. It places pain in the heart of God.[13]

But it is this pain which gives birth to joy – to healing, to justice, to hope, to wholeness, to salvation and release from all that enslaves and corrupts.

8 COMPASSION

Compassion has been banished. It is in exile. Everywhere there is evidence of lack of thought, care and concern for one another and for the planet. Air, water and earth have been polluted and poisoned. The Earth is scarred and mutilated. We are indifferent to what we do – or fail to do – to one another. Thus, misery of every sort is compounded. And it is hard to believe that we truly care for our children when our present actions make it so unlikely that their children will have a world worth living in. We live in a time of unprecedented human suffering.

The knowledge and ability to do something about such suffering are often not available. We still do not know, for example, how to produce and distribute enough food for the world's growing population. Most of us can list the crises: environmental, ecological, population, North/South, East/West, urbanisation, terrorism and violence of every sort. And the suffering continues to worsen. More knowledge, resources and research are needed. But at the level of will and motivation, something is lacking. And that is compassion. Meanwhile we are all dying from the lack of it, and surrendering our humanity together.

But the word 'compassion' is still in use. Politicians attack each other for not being compassionate or caring. Towards the end of the British general election campaign in 1979, Neil Kinnock attacked the Prime Minister for not being compassionate. Politicians have more access to the media than anyone else. They are among the leading opinion-formers and attitude-changers. Their use of words, particularly of a semi-religious word like 'compassion', is therefore significant.

In general usage, being compassionate means bothering or caring about someone. But that is to reduce and diminish its meaning – because it invariably conceals an attitude which can be patronising and condescending. We talk about 'taking pity on' someone. The preposition 'on' fosters the illusion of distance and separateness; a few more crumbs will be handed out. More resources will be 'targeted' to the weak and vulnerable, but those who are doing the handing out remain untouched and unmoved. Their wealth remains intact. When, in the cold winter of 1986/87, St James's Church, Piccadilly, opened its doors to the homeless (both old and young), a rich widow rang me and said she would ask her staff to send down some soup, if that would help.

Sometimes apparent compassion is little more than gloating at someone else's plight. This is a type of vicarious masochism which finds satisfaction by feeling another's pain, emphasising the distance between the persons involved. Then compassion is understood as a private, inward, self-indulgent sentiment brought about momentarily by a pang of conscience. And its very inwardness destroys the energy and ability to act.

None of these perceptions of compassion reflect its true meaning. Thomas Merton, the American monk and spiritual teacher, in an address just before he died, said that 'The whole idea of compassion is based on a keen awareness of the interdependence of all living beings which are all part of one another, and are all involved in one another.'[1] Time and again I have used the words 'interdependence' and 'mutuality'. (It is regrettable that we do not have less abstract and more direct words to describe the interrelatedness of everything.) They express the heart of compassion from which tenderness towards others, as well as toughness and resistance to injustice, flow.

The photographs that astronauts have taken of the Earth bring interdependence, interrelatedness, interconnectedness, to life. The biologist Lewis Thomas writes: 'Viewed from the distance of the moon, the astonishing thing about the earth, catching the breath, is that it is alive . . . the rising earth, the only exuberant thing in this part of the cosmos.' He goes on to say that 'the earth is like a simple cell. We should credit it for what it is: for sheer size and perfection of function it is far and away the grandest collaboration of nature.'[2]

Compassion should be perceived initially on this global scale. Then it can operate from a bond of shared strength and shared weakness. A compassionate person recognises that we are all in this world – a global village – together. A compassionate person is one who knows, shares, enters and tastes as far as he or she is able, the pain of the other. They have an acute awareness of our common heritage, our shared existence with the rest of Creation and of its richness, complexity and extravagant diversity. They sense the universal presence of this grace. And this awareness transcends all differences and divisions.

Some years ago, a minister in Washington DC invited the city's dozen wealthiest men to meet and have a meal with a dozen representatives of the poor in inner-city Washington. The preparation for this unusual event was difficult. The rich prevaricated. Perhaps in six months' time or so, when their diaries were less full; anyhow, most of them already did a lot for the poor. Were they not trustees of some of the most prestigious foundations in the USA who allocated funds for the relief of poverty? And they were always being badgered for funds. The poor were suspicious. Were they going to be patronised? And the fixing of the date became an issue. Union leaders of the unemployed or of tenants' associations do not need to fix a meeting six months in advance.

The purpose of the meal was for the rich to listen to the experiences of the poor. The evening began with much mutual suspicion in spite of all the patient preparation by the minister and his staff. Eventually the atmosphere changed. And by the time everyone had helped to clear the tables and done the washing-up together, much of the earlier suspicion and wariness had evaporated.

What happened was simple. As the rich listened, so they began to see through the eyes of the speakers something of their dignity, resilience, anger, shame, vitality and courage. Their humanity called out of them the beginnings of understanding and respect. They did not immediately write out cheques for the projects for which the assistance was required. But in the weeks and months which followed, some funds were released, expertise and skills were provided and, as a result, schemes for the rehabilitation of homes in inner-city Washington and elsewhere have taken shape. In some cases, mutual trust has developed between the parties concerned, and the wealthy have become the learners.

This is a story of how compassion begins to flower. And a feature of that meal together was that by the end of the evening it had become a celebration. It was not just a question of troubles shared, troubles halved; but of joys shared, joys doubled. The rich, who had to listen, were able to celebrate their humanity – which they shared with the poor. The wealthy businessmen recognised a bleakness, a lack of vitality and energy in their own lives (in spite, or because, of the pressures to keep on becoming more successful, to keep their complex operations under control). But they noticed the energy, clarity, passion and vitality of those who told their stories. For a time in that simple dining room, it might have been said that joy was an appropriate response, because the occasion celebrated the need each had for the other. There is no compassion without celebration. After all, there is no possibility for celebration when someone at a distance expresses pity for someone else.

On 19 February 1988 the Rt Revd Michael Baughen, Bishop of Chester, addressed his diocesan synod on homosexuality. The summary of his speech, recorded by his Communications Officer, says:

> The bishop demonstrated how . . . there can be compassion towards homosexuality seen as a symptom of the secular world turning away from God, and there can also be compassion towards

Christians who are homosexual by orientation, but who refuse to practise genital acts because of their faith.

Previously, at the November synod of the Church of England, the Bishop proposed an amendment to the Reverend Tony Highton's motion on sexual morality. In contrast to the uncompromising and fierce tone of the Highton proposal, the Bishop proposed that 'homosexual genital acts that fall short of this ideal are to be met by a call to repentance and the exercise of compassion'.

Phrases like 'showing' or 'exercising compassion' suggest that the Bishop wanted to take pity on homosexuals or he may have felt sorry for them. But would he be prepared to celebrate with them? Celebration means being with them, sharing in the love and concern which homosexuals show one for another – and that in itself is an example to the rest of us. Would he be able to hold a young man dying of Aids in his arms? Would he be prepared, as the rich Washington men were, to listen to the poor, to listen to the homosexuals tell of their shame, of their anger and rejection by the Church? Would he then, if he was invited, be prepared to sit and eat and celebrate with them? If so, he, and others like him, could be called compassionate. Otherwise, whether or not a bishop, priest, or anyone else considers they are compassionate, they are mistaken.

There are deliberate resonances with the Gospels in the last paragraph. What angered the authorities and shocked Jesus's contemporaries was the way he ate with the 'scum' of Palestinian society: the poor of every sort, the beggars, the crippled, the prostitutes, the tax collectors and the illiterate. He was regarded as a 'glutton and drunkard, a friend of tax collectors and sinners'. For Jesus (being regarded as a holy man, rabbi, teacher and prophet), sharing food and drink with such people was profoundly scandalous in a society where much attention was paid to ritual purity before meals were taken. Jesus made those who accepted the offer to eat with him (and his offer was always inclusive) strong, cleansed, healthy and whole. His 'guests' were restored to their dignity and humanity. This inclusive table fellowship was a sign of, and a result of, the compassion of Jesus – a key word in the early accounts of his ministry.

Thus, in Mathew 14:14, 'Jesus . . . was moved with compassion towards them, and he healed the sick.' And in Matthew 9:36, '. . . he was moved with compassion on them, because they fainted, and were scattered abroad, as a sheep having no shepherd.' Luke 7:13 tells us that '. . . when the Lord saw her [the widow of Nain], he had compassion on her, and said unto her, Weep not.' In Mark 1:40–42, we learn that he had compassion on a leper; on two blind men in Matthew 20:34; and on those who had nothing to eat in Matthew 20:82. He often says: Do not cry; do not be afraid; do not worry.

The Greek word for 'compassion' is hardly translatable into English – hence the awkwardness of the phrase 'moved to compassion'. It means that compassion is a reaction from both gut *and* heart; it means embracing the feeling or situation of another. To be moved to compassion is to absorb the pain of another.

Although compassion speaks from the heart and to the heart, there is, in the Gospels, a public and political aspect to the word. The people were 'harassed and helpless' – that is to say, others were harassing them; they were being made helpless. They were hungry, not through their own fault, but because of the repressive political system under which the Jewish people lived at the time. (The stories of the miraculous feeding of the crowd reflect the concern of Jesus's disciples that they had so little food to share.) Empires or democracies are not organised on the basis of compassion. Therefore, when Jesus showed compassion (and that must have been a precious memory about him when the Gospels were being assembled), he was making a public stand – a public criticism of all authorities which try to ignore or repress grief, pain and suffering.

Further exploration in this direction would focus on the Jewish Christian's emphasis on compassion, not as sentiment but as action – in feeding, sheltering, clothing, forgiving, healing, setting free. And such actions are invariably related to justice: putting relationships right, and pursuing the goal of a fair distribution of resources. In other words these actions put into practice the basic principle of sharing which Jesus refers to so persistently in his warnings to the rich.

Christianity certainly does not have a monopoly on compassion. It is a fundamental teaching of all major religions. In the Koran it says: 'There is not an animal on earth, nor a flying creature on two wings but they are people like you.'[3] The same is true of Hinduism. The great fourth-century BC epic poem, the *Mahabharata*, tells us: 'We bow to all beings with great reverence in the thought and knowledge that God enters into them through fractioning himself as a living creature.'[4]

In view of this prominence of compassion in all religions, why has it now been exiled? The story of Jacob's ladder in Genesis 28:10-19 may provide the answer:

> And Jacob went out from Beersheba, and went toward Haran. And he lighted upon a certain place, and tarried there all night, because the sun was set; and he took of the stones of that place, and put them for his pillows, and lay down in that place to sleep. And he dreamed, and behold a ladder set up on the earth, and the top of it reached to heaven: and behold the angels of God ascending and descending on it. And, behold, the Lord stood above it, and said, I am the Lord God of Abraham thy father, and the God of Isaac: the land whereon thou liest, to thee will I give it, and to thy seed; and thy seed shall be as the dust of the earth, and thou shalt spread abroad to the west, and to the east, and to the north, and to the south: and in thee and in thy seed shall all the families of the earth be blessed. And, behold, I am with thee, and will keep thee in all places whither thou goest, and will bring thee again into this land; for I will not leave thee, until I have done that which I have spoken to thee of. And Jacob awaked out of his sleep, and he said, Surely the Lord is in this place; and I knew it not. And he was afraid, and said, How dreadful is this place! this is none other but the house of God, and this is the gate of heaven.

> And Jacob rose up early in the morning, and took the stone that he had put for his pillows, and set it up for a pillar, and poured oil upon the top of it. And he called the name of that place Bethel: but the name of that city was called Luz at the first.

This story has influenced many Christian writers on the Christian character; the ladder is an archetypal metaphor for our ascent to God. Even those who have never read the literature about the ladder will have been influenced by it.

In its Jewish context the story is simple and profound. Jacob stands alone; his sole purpose is survival. But in the dream, a new reality breaks in. He is assured of God's presence with him always; this dream contradicts all despairing judgements about human existence. It is an astonishing disclosure that God will take his place with this man, whose life is threatened by his brother Esau. God's promise is to 'keep' or protect him; Israel will not be left to its own devices. And the last element in the story is the promise of homecoming after exile. Presence, promise and homecoming are surprising aspects of the good news which needed the device of a dream to bring out their significant character.

This interpretation is not the one familiar to the Church. The ladder image was taken over as a metaphor for the way to God by male theologians writing about the spiritual life. This meant that in order to reach God, it was necessary to flee the Earth (meaning Nature), other people, the sensual and the physical. The image was about the journey upwards, away from the Earth. This literature did not deal with the journey downwards to the Earth and to people, where compassion may be found. Gregory of Nyssa writes:

> It was the virtuous life which was shown to the Patriarch under the figure of the ladder, in order that he himself might learn and also impart to his descendants that one can ascend to God only if one always looks upwards. . . . Jacob saw God enthroned upon a ladder.[5]

The consequences of the ladder image, as misinterpreted by St Gregory and others, have been devastating. Looking up – in worship – also means to shut up; in other words, to put up with whatever has to be put up with. Staying down and looking up encourages the unhealthy veneration of saints, holy persons and others whom we are encouraged to emulate. To practise such pedestal piety has the effect of denying our capacity for taking responsibility.

But the ladder image has significant social, psychological and political consequences which ensure that the door is kept firmly locked against compassion. The ladder encourages the worst aspects of competition. There is no compassion when a person is driven by the need for power, possessions or prestige. Gratitude and laughter are not found. The ladder image inevitably means that only a few reach the top, and the higher they go, the more dangerous it becomes, so they make every effort to hold on tight. (No hands are free to help those on the lowest rungs.) Those who reach the top are those who say what is what. (From the top of a skyscraper, the people on the streets seem tiny, insignificant and of no account.) And since the ascent is to God, who is the judge, God's justice is exerted over those below and is tempered by mercy. (This, incidentally, is a travesty of justice according to the Christian tradition which speaks of the rich being judged by God, and God as the saviour of the poor.)

The ladder image encourages elitism and the survival of the fittest; it creates hierarchies. The top rungs of the ladder are made 'sacred'. The ladder image has no place for Creation – for the Earth or for the world of animals – which accounts for the thoughtless and cruel way in which both Nature and animals are treated. The ladder image emphasises separateness and the making of distinctions. It encourages those on the ladder to get away from all that binds us together, and focus on their own individual ascent to a distant, abstract, cold and formal God.

There is, however, another image from the book of Genesis which is more pertinent for the living of a compassionate life, and that is Sarah's circle. Genesis 18:11–15 tells us that Sarah was 90 and Abraham 100 when she heard that she would have a child:

> Now Abraham and Sarah were old and well stricken in age; and it ceased to be with Sarah after the manner of women. Therefore Sarah laughed within herself, saying, After I am waxed old shall I have pleasure, my lord being old also? And the Lord said unto Abraham, Wherefore did Sarah laugh, saying, Shall I of a surety bear a child, which am old? Is any thing too hard for the Lord? At

the time appointed I will return unto thee, according to the time of life, and Sarah shall have a son. Then Sarah denied, saying, I laughed not; for she was afraid. And he said, Nay; but thou didst laugh.

And so it happened, as we are told in Genesis 21:1–7:

And the Lord visited Sarah as he had said, and the Lord did unto Sarah as he had spoken. For Sarah conceived, and bare Abraham a son in his old age, at the set time of which God had spoken to him. And Abraham called the name of his son that was born unto him, whom Sara bare to him, Isaac. And Abraham circumcised his son Isaac being eight days old, as God had commanded him. And Abraham was an hundred years old, when his son Isaac was born unto him. And Sarah said, God hath made me to laugh, so that all that hear will laugh with me. And she said, Who would have said unto Abraham, that Sarah should have given children suck? for I have born him a son in his old age.

The name Isaac, Sarah's afterthought son, means 'God has smiled, God has been kind'.

The circle is not mentioned in the Genesis account, but it is an apt description of a community gathered round to witness an astonishing act of creativity. The invention of this symbol is recent, and by women, so theologians have not yet considered it. If the ladder image seems so secure, so fixed, so much an account of the way things are that it can barely be questioned, Sarah's circle offers something quite different. It says that the universe is not reliable or stable or closed, but that God can shatter all known certainties, and break through death, hopelessness and barrenness to offer a promise of a more human and humane future. It is a story about faith being accommodated – a story about the most astonishing new prospects before the human race if only they could see them. The reaction to this news is laughter; in the Old Testament that is always the reaction to some phenomenon which cannot be explained.

Sarah's circle is one of laughter and joy, and the cause of her laughter is her pregnancy. Her giving birth, her creativity and fruitfulness are signs of the creativity and fruitfulness of God;

God's nearness in one of the most mysterious human actions. Those who participate in Sarah's circle at least begin to make sense of the shape of the universe. No one puts a ladder on a sphere (which is something like the shape of the universe we inhabit).

Moving up and down implies a flat surface, a flat Earth. But the Earth is curved. Pilots speak of flying in and out of different altitudes. Those who join Sarah's circle fly in, as it were, to enjoy the Earth, the sensuality, the beauty and delights of Creation, and fly out to see how they can fashion a more just, peaceful and wholesome world reflecting unity and beauty. An 'in and out' rather than an 'up and down' perception is appropriate for a nuclear, ecological age where taking responsibility for one another and every living thing is crucial.

Whereas the ladder implies the arduous, solo effort of climbing, in the circle all dance together, supporting and encouraging one another. And since the circle is never closed, helping hands are always inviting God's 'little ones' to join in: the physically and mentally handicapped, the elderly and whoever in our own day is regarded as the 'scum' of society.

One of my most precious memories of Sarah's circle in action occurred at a wedding party I attended on a South London housing estate where I worked. Mrs Smith was in her late seventies. She had spent 15 years or so in a wheelchair. I knew her well, and others knew that she could walk a few steps. The party was an old-fashioned 'knees-up' with dancing in which all could join, irrespective of age. Some wedding parties on the estate used to end unpleasantly with much drunkenness and self-recrimination. But this particular occasion was rather different.

We were all dancing 'The Dashing White Sergeant' when I noticed Mrs Smith's two grandsons leave the floor and go up to her. With difficulty and much grace, they persuaded her to stand and take a few steps and join us in our celebration. I doubt that anyone present will forget that moment when, supported by her grandchildren, she stood up, left the security of her wheelchair and joined us all. In the circle, there is always room for others. And if the circle gets too large, then it is easy to split into smaller circles.

The circle dance depends on the interaction and interdependence of all. There is no room for individualism. In the world of the ladder, there is gossip, bitchiness and envy; in the circle dance energy is spent in doing one's part, and sustaining and encouraging one another. There is no hierarchy. The eye-contact each makes with the other points towards a truly equal democracy, but one that still recognises the unique gifts and talents of each. Circle dancing is a physical activity. There is sweat, the touching of hands and bodies, close and necessary contact with the Earth – far removed from the chilling, thin air inhabited by those on the top of the ladder. In Sarah's circle, compassion finds its true home.[6]

Abraham Herschel wrote:

> God created a reminder, an image;
> Humanity is a reminder of God.
> As God is compassionate,
> Let humanity be compassionate.[7]

The compassion of humanity will blossom in Sarah's circle. Compassion is the richest energy source, and the potential for compassion lies within all of us. Sarah's circles exist today only in small ways. But they are of great worth, and for those who participate in them they are often a matter of life and death. I am thinking of groups like Alcoholics Anonymous, and the many interest groups which have developed on the same principles. They provide examples of interdependence, occasions where each can look into the eyes of another without self-pity, support without sentimentality, and opportunities to move away from the shadow of the ladder to live a day at a time rather than being driven ever upwards and onwards.

Some of the most altruistic and compassionate people I know are alcoholics who have been helped by the group without any compensation and who have been allowed to express their compulsiveness and frustrations without recrimination. It is freedom and security which allow these changes to occur. Compassion is to be found in the most unlikely places.

Compassion is present when Creation is respected. At the most ordinary level, a good gardener is compassionate towards Creation. The gardener knows the importance of patience. Nothing can be hurried. Words like 'manipulation' and 'control' are not in the gardener's vocabulary. The Earth is a sacred place; we are of the Earth, and to the Earth we shall return. When the tough, gentle and compassionate St Francis was dying he asked to be laid naked on the Earth. Francis died 'singing' and he wanted to be placed on his 'Sister Earth, our Mother', as he called it in the 'Canticle of the Sun'.

The Earth is not inanimate. It is a mass of living things eating one another in order to make the soil a viable environment for other forms of life. We are as dependent on the Earth as the tiniest of insects. Plants need soil; animals need plants; and humankind needs them all – earth, insects, plants and animals – for our own survival. All are interdependent, for the Earth is never to be plundered ruthlessly, else it will die, and we in time will die with it. There is no compassion without humility towards the Earth. Gardeners with green fingers will know all this instinctively – they will know something of the mysteries of the Earth as the soil slips through their fingers.

In the light of the problems the world faces, these examples of compassion may seem too small and trivial to alter anything. But the places and occasions where compassion is found are bound to be modest since it has been almost totally repressed and banished. Ultimately compassion offers the key to a new politics and a new economics in the face of threats from ecological disasters and the possibility of a nuclear holocaust. It finds its home wherever interdependence and interrelatedness occur in a context of equality and celebration, and this provides a sign as to how we should relate to one another and the planet.

The working out of compassion as the key to co-operation, collaboration and justice is far beyond the scope of this book. But given the emphasis on compassion found in all major religions of the world, perhaps a start could be made with a global, ecumenical initiative to explore its implications and depths of meaning.

Compassion is an almost lost, but beautiful, powerful, vibrant experience full of possibilities and hope for us all. Jacob's ladder and Sarah's circle – it is not possible to be on the ladder and in the circle at once. Put one foot on the ladder and one in the circle – and the result will be most uncomfortable. Sooner or later a choice has to be made!

9 TOGETHER?

'Life is suffering.' This is the first of the Four Noble Truths taught by Buddha. Perhaps another way to say this is that life is difficult. Most of us do not recognise this fundamental truth. We moan more or less continually about our problems, our burdens, other people and the world in general. The assumption behind all this complaining is that life should be easy. If only, I say – for I do my share of moaning – this or that problem would go away or be solved, preferably by someone else, life would become easy.

Is Life Meant to be Easy?

We are encouraged to believe that life should be problem-free. The iconographers of this false consciousness are the advertisers who seek to persuade us that the right car, coffee, after-shave or beer will ensure love and happiness. This advertising is so relentless, unavoidable and sophisticated that it becomes quite difficult to insist that its promises are illusory. Might the advertisers be right after all?

Experience proves otherwise. We expect and hope that life will become easier, but that is not necessarily so. After 12 years as a vicar in a South London housing estate I thought I needed to move to another job. I felt like a whale in a fish pond. As an ambitious young clergyman, I wondered whether I would be asked to be a bishop. I set about enlisting support from my friends. If only I could secure this or that job, I remember saying, all my problems would be over.

It was then that the Bishop of London invited me to become Rector of St James's Church, Piccadilly. My problems were over. I went on a marvellous Californian holiday and life was easy. But when I started at St James's I discovered a minute congregation and a church which was more or less bankrupt. I was faced with more problems. Once they were solved others would emerge, and so it has continued. It is absurd to think that life should by rights be trouble-free, but such a notion still persists.

I should have known better. Some 20 years before, I had been involved in a difficult relationship. It played havoc with my public as well as my private life. I felt trapped, but it was not an altogether unpleasurable experience: the pain of loving someone too much was at least familiar. But I also longed to be free of it. Sometimes my anger with myself and the other person was frightening in its intensity. Our relationship staggered on. I hoped it might one day just come to an end. I spent a lot of energy rationalising and explaining it away. Eventually I sought professional help and began to see that avoiding problems, and the suffering in them, is the root of all mental illness. Many of us go to the most extraordinary lengths to avoid having to face problems. And this denial and cover-up leads to neurosis, which Jung said is 'always a substitute for legitimate suffering'.

It was also during this time that I began to feel stuck. I had ceased to grow, and felt as if I were going round and round in circles. It was not until I faced up to the cause of my problems in the counselling process that the obsession began to disappear, and my spirit started to return. The counselling itself was painful. It took some courage to bring to the light distant, bad, memories which needed healing, in the hope that they would no longer have power over me.

The purpose of telling these stories – both quite un-
exceptional – is to remind myself and others not only that life is
never problem-free, but that pain and legitimate suffering have
to be faced up to, dealt with and understood, so that development and growth are not impeded. To assist in this
necessary confrontation of pain, one has to find a discipline or a
way to promote healthy growth and development.

The Quest for Holiness

There is an additional factor which broadens the
context of any discipline and this is the quest for holiness. Holiness is a prompting from God to undertake the religious journey. It is a quest for wholeness, to realise the extraordinary
assertion that each of us is made in the image of God. It is
almost invariably the example of another which triggers the
desire to be like that person who, in his or her simplicity and
transparency, discloses something of God.

I think of Lill Alexander. Her son, Terry, was dying of Aids.
He was the subject of one of the first television documentaries
about Aids. But it was Terry's mother, Lill, who I remember. In
spite of a stroke, and two heart attacks, Lill made a two-hour
journey to be with her son each day. She was not worried that
he was gay. 'I knew before he did,' she said. Her visits showed
her care, respect and affection for her son. She did everything
she could for him.

One day Terry noticed she was crying a little. He asked why.
She pulled herself together, wiped her tears away and said, 'I
have really got nothing to cry about. There are others worse
than me.' Lill also had a daughter suffering from Down's syn-
drome: 'I had her when I was 47. They said, "Why didn't you
have an abortion?" ' She explained, 'My first husband was really
good to me. I can't do that to him.'

I have no idea whether Lill Alexander has any religious
beliefs. I expect she would consider any talk about a quest for
holiness as pretentious. All I know is I wish I had something of

her generosity, courage, toughness, clarity and warmth. Her great humanity is an example of wholeness.

I think of Mahatma Gandhi. There are many stories about him, not all of them flattering. But of his holiness there is one which is particularly telling. When he came to London in 1931 for the Round Table Conference, Gandhi wanted to meet Mary Hughes, a social worker living in the East End of London. She was well known for her service to the poor and she lived a life of much frugality. The only day they were both free was on the day of the week that Gandhi kept silence. That was fine, said Mary Hughes. They met – in silence. They smiled and looked at one another. They left each other mutually and considerably enriched.

The beginning of the way to holiness may be an involuntary – almost unconscious – step, inspired by the example and practice of others. But sometimes it can be quite simple and direct. Donald Nicholl, in his classic study *Holiness*, tells the story of Thich Nhat Hanh, a Vietnamese Buddhist priest. During a lecture at an American university he was asked a question about meditation: 'Could you tell us how you meditate in your monastery in Vietnam?' To this, Thich Nhat Hanh replied, 'In our monastery no one is allowed to meditate until he has spent at least three years learning how to serve tea to the older monks.'[1] Certainly, take one step towards God, and as an Indian saying has it, God takes 10 steps towards you. The quest for holiness, for union with God, is terrifying – everything is in question. It is a costly pilgrimage.

Christianity has produced a range of techniques, aids, and libraries of advice on how to become holy; some of this, as I will show shortly, is inappropriate. There still lingers the notion that holiness is a special characteristic of saints. The Roman Catholic Church once encouraged the belief that saints were those who had transcended ordinary human existence. They embodied the ideals of purity, goodness, and self-sacrifice – far removed from the experience of most people.

Ascetic practices were common among saints, from Simon Stylites who perched on the top of a pillar for the last 30 years of his life, to a number of child saints who fasted from breast-feeding on days of penitence before festivals. In a hierarchical church with pope, bishop, priests, and then men and women, there was a tendency to associate holiness with social rank. Many saints were therefore of 'good family'. Sacrifice was an important traditional path to holiness, but the reversal of worldly status was that much easier and more impressive if the person was a noble and not a peasant!

The popular criteria for holiness would have included evidence of miraculous powers whereby the person was able to interrupt the course of Nature through miracles of healing and cure. They would possess almost 'magical' qualities, such as clairvoyance – the 'reading' of hearts so that character could be quickly assessed. They were expected to be exemplary in self-denial: performing every sort of penance, practising self-flagellation and making pilgrimages on their knees. The vows of chastity were regarded as very honourable because the temptation of the flesh stood in the way of union with God. The saints would be known for their humility, predilection for solitude and reluctance to be seen in public. But they would also be expected to pray continually for the world, and their presence was understood as an evangelical sign. Those who were canonised tended to be priests and founders of religious orders; 87 per cent of saints are men; 13 per cent are women. And there is a conspicuous absence of married lay saints, since marriage has traditionally been considered inferior to chastity.

This may be a caricature of the way holiness has been understood and practised. It is easy to mock, and it is therefore important to remember that the Roman Catholic Church has also sanctified many women and men who exemplified the humanity of a contemporary like Lill Alexander.

But many of these ascetic practices – the split between body and spirit, the fear of and aversion to sexuality and to women – do not foster lives of fullness and wholeness. It is just not possible to leave the treadmill of guilt where such dualism and loathing of the body exists.

My own diaries at the time I became a Christian reflect this no-win situation. If the object was to get closer to God by praying, studying the scriptures, going to church, doing without sleep, fasting and going to confession, I had no chance of succeeding. I had to do more and more to placate God's anger for all my anxiety and guilt about so many things.

The more I tried and failed, the worse I felt. Then I became aware that I was committing the very worst sin of all – pride. And it was back to the treadmill again. In my early days as a Christian I had begun to control all my desires, aspirations and enthusiasms which had previously been so crucial to my life. In the quest for holiness there is therefore a necessary unlearning process, in which we begin to see how wrong many of our attitudes have been, to what we see, taste, experience and feel. Then we acquire some of the right ones – attitudes which will help, not hinder, us in our journey.

Once embarked, the first task is to come to terms with our own mortality. It is one of the less obvious signs of Christianity's absorption into the values of capitalism and materialism that Christians behave as if life were to go on for ever and ever. The absence of any sense of the fragile and transitory nature of each of our lives is a sure sign of loss of belief in God. Even though death is such a visible and massive presence around us, it is always someone else who dies! As a friend told me, who had just been informed that he had only a year to live, 'I didn't think that was possible because I have such a full diary.'

One of the tasks of a minister of religion is to officiate at funerals. This invariably involves a spell of duty at a cemetery or crematorium. Sometimes there might be seven or eight funerals in one day. It is a dispiriting and discouraging experience because there is no chance of meeting the mourners properly or knowing anything about the person lying in the coffin. So that cold November afternoon in a drab South London municipal cemetery – my fourth funeral that day – was particularly remarkable. As I committed the body to the ground – earth to earth, dust to dust – i noticed a muddy puddle, a dirty green rhododendron bush whose leaves were splattered with mud thrown up by the funeral cars, the haphazard pattern of the stones and ground, and the movement of a few birds. They were all suddenly so precious and so beautiful that for a moment I felt grateful to be alive. Instead of feeling bored and tired, and wondering (as I usually did) how many more funerals I had to do that day, I felt exhilarated. There, in that cheerless place, I experienced a wonder of Creation and realised how little time we each occupy in it.

Meditation on our own death can easily lead to the worst sort of other-worldly religion. In days when people believed that prayers and pious activities could ensure a place in heaven, the wealthy could rest assured that their journey would be undisturbed by their privileged lives. For the poor, life could only improve after death, so meanwhile they would remember their lowly place in society and act accordingly.

But, as in my experience in the cemetery, coming to terms with dying can create a clearer perception of Creation and a freer attitude towards possessions. Shortly after the cemetery incident I was invited to a dinner party. All the people (except myself) were of substantial means. And much of the conversation was about the burden their properties in various parts of the world were creating. Should they sell this one or that one? What was one to do with the properties when they were empty? Security was a nightmare, as was the servant problem.

I was happy to take a back seat in the conversation, and I was therefore surprised when my host suddenly asked me what I should do? I had the chance either to be quite noncommital (I had no experience of their problems) or to try and shift the conversation. So I said, 'Well, I certainly sympathise with your situation, but I think I would remind myself that everything we have is on loan from God. Nothing is ours; all is on loan, even the people and the things which are most precious to us.' The conversation changed!

Wherever I have met holiness or aspects of holiness in people who would not consider themselves holy, or even religious, it is shown in this freedom towards material things, and what I can only describe as a transparency in their being because they have turned towards the light – the light of their dying. Such people – particularly those who have come to accept terminal illness – are deeply healthy, integrated and life-giving to those who care for them. This is because they have acquired a love, respect and sense of wonder at Creation which many of them had probably repressed since childhood.

Repressing this wonder helps to kill our capacity for holiness, and begins to destroy a proper sense of humility. Wendell Berry, in his essay 'The Body and the Earth', wrote:

> The creation is bounteous and mysterious, and humanity is only a part of it . . . not its equal, much less its master . . . the creation provides a place for humans, but it is greater than humanity and within it even great men are small. Such humanity is the consequence of an accurate insight, ecological in its bearing, not a pious deference to 'spiritual value'.[2]

Elsewhere in this book we have discussed the need to find new ways of talking about God which will enable us to take responsibility for Creation and for one another. The prospect of our dying may enlarge our capacity to be responsible, and to perceive Creation as a gift. From this standpoint, our task is to be co-creators with God, fashioned as we are in the image of God.

Taking responsibility sounds formidable, and it certainly is, because of the possibilities of destruction if we fail. But it is also a most direct and intimate requirement: each member of the human race is a recipient of the gift of the universe over 19 million years; each of us brings together in our bodies all the pain and travail of the creatures who have in the long history of evolution given their lives for us. Because of this we can be responsible for what we eat, for what we see, for what we hear and for what we say. We can use or misuse our bodies. They can be turned into machines, as athletes sometimes do; or they can be ignored as if we were merely talking heads, until parts of them cease to work, and the whole body is affected. All the major religions have regulations or advice about food, fasting, abstinence and use and abuse of sexuality. They point to the most direct form of responsibility – concern for our bodies.

On the way to holiness, we have identified one feature of the necessary discipline – being responsible. Problems can only be solved by solving them. This statement may be obvious but it is lost on many of us because of the difficulty of accepting responsibility for a problem before it is solved. Some religions say that ultimately God takes care of everything, and this belief reinforces the view of those who say that it is not their problem – it was caused by others, by society – it was nothing to do with them.

There is real pain in discovering freedom, in having to make choices. And our impotence and sense of helplessness and uselessness often arise from having given that power away, and having turned ourselves into victims. To the extent that each person can take responsibility for his or her life, and for one another, growth is not hindered and healing can take place.

Reflection

One of the reasons why counselling is becoming a fast-growing middle-class industry is simply that it is one of the few forums left where it is possible to engage in the necessary human process of reflecting. Reflection is a process in which we attend to what is going on within us, and around us. This does not happen as often as it could because our lives are too hurried. An accident, illness, bereavement, divorce, the break-up of a relationship, redundancy, retirement – these interruptions in 'normal' living are often the only occasions when we pause, reflect and look at what is happening. A marriage guidance counsellor's first question is: Are you both talking to one another? And talking, in this context, means at least trying to listen to the other person's point of view.

Socrates said that an unexamined life is not worth living; the same mistakes are made over and over again. There is no awareness of the effect our behaviour has on other people, and life seems to be little more than a random series of events, as opposed to a story which may reflect a little of the grace and love of God. Without reflection, life stagnates, and the human spirit shrivels.

Sooner or later, anyone who has embarked on the way of holiness has to discover how to engage in reflection. There are many ways but all religions have one way in common and that is silence. Prayer, meditation, contemplation – or even just sitting and breathing – are some of the activities that religious people engage in when they seek to bring their lives to God. Silence is necessary and golden, because it can stir the imagination to the call of holiness.

But silence is a difficult art to learn because of the business and hurry of living. Try sitting and doing nothing for five minutes. After a minute or so, the body will begin to get restless and the mind will dart about, rushing from image to image. It feels as if we are trying to catch up with ourselves. That is the result of hurry, which is caused by the inordinate desire to have more, do more and be more – to fit in everything so none of our time is wasted. Replete with information (if that is what we are seeking) or many friends (if that is what we need) or many varied experiences (if that is what seems right), there is no time left in our lives for reflection. And when, as happens sooner or later, something goes badly wrong, there are few tools around to help us interpret and make sense of our experience.

This is not the place to consider the various forms of prayer. But one form is significant because it involves facing and confronting pain. By pain I do not mean toothache or minor inconveniences, I mean experiences which destroy familiar landmarks: redundancy, break-up of relationships, failure in projects, conflicts and confusions of all sorts. Occasionally, as I have discovered, a religious dimension emerges from these traumatic experiences, particularly if there is someone close at hand who knows how to handle this type of situation.

There is a type of prayer which does not rely on words. It is a prayer of contemplation in which the mind, body and spirit let go. It is a prayer of trust; and the literature which describes it speaks of drowning, sinking and darkness.

I was 'programmed' as a little boy to be frightened of the dark. I had to have the landing light on, and my bedroom door open – just in case. Yet growth of any sort needs the dark. Our bodies function just as well in the dark as they do in the day. Most of us were conceived in the dark, and for nine months we experienced the warmth and safety of the womb. Darkness need not be so disturbing. The poet Rainer Rilke understood darkness well:

> You darkness, that I come from, I love you more than all the fires that fence in the world, for the fire makes a circle of light for everyone, and then no one outside you.
>
> But the darkness pulls in everything:
> shapes and fires, animals and myself
> how easily it gathers them!
> power and people –
> And it is possible a great energy
> is moving near me.
> I have faith in nights.[3]

Rilke's experience is very different from that of most of us. It takes a lot of courage to trust the pain, and the darkness in which it is enclosed. The befriending of pain is a little like loving your enemies, as Jesus urged his followers to do. And the only reason for trusting, and not panicking, is that many who have followed this path before us speak hesitatingly and clearly of God within this pain. That is how to speak of healing which happens slowly, and in fits and starts. Of course, there are many ways of describing this healing process – from a psychological or scientific perspective. But for me, Rilke's description of letting go into nothingness and into God describes the experience most fully and accurately.

The energies that pain provides are those which assist us to grow as compassionate women and men. To have suffered once and deeply is an experience never forgotten, and once that suffering has been faced it is difficult for that person to ignore the suffering of others.

A good friend of mine who has led a privileged life nevertheless suffers from an ailment which places him in permanent discomfort. But over the years he has come to see that his physical pain is a means by which he can identify himself with those who are made to feel ashamed and humiliated. When pain is shared and acknowledged, then whether it is personal, social or political – like injustice – it can be resolved. And such people are well on the way to holiness, because they have known and experienced the presence of God in places where despair seems to hold sway.

Collective Holiness

So far the quest for holiness has been described in personal and private terms. Taking responsibility, confronting pain, meditating on death, thanking God for the gift of life and Creation – these are some of the essential activities which any-one striving for holiness should undertake. But to understand it in such an individualistic manner is to reduce the meaning and experience of holiness. After all, one of the principal themes of this book is our growing awareness of the interdependence of everything, and of the complexity and beauty of the world. There is therefore a sense in which all creatures and human communities are called to be holy. It is a visionary concept, relying on a sense of the transfiguration of everything in God. It requires us to realise that every aspect of Creation has within it the possibility of development into a far greater potential. It means acknowledging that the process of evolution is unfinished.

We are a long way from such a vision being realised. I find it easier to speak metaphorically of the way in which the Earth is being crucified, and has become the victim of all victims. We have seen Bhopal and Chernobyl. There is deforestation and pollution. There is the disappearance of living species at the rate of one every 25 minutes. (There are some 10 million living species. At this rate, there will be none left in 100 years, not even humankind.) There is the dumping of dangerous chemicals and nuclear waste deep in the Earth. A dying Earth has become the victim of our callous, indifferent and arrogant hands – hardly a likely locale for the holiness of God.

Holiness for Creation may become a reality when its desecration is truly acknowledged, and repentance and lamentation take place, followed by a shift in the way in which all human life is perceived. Matthew Fox, in *The Coming of the Cosmic Christ*, quotes the scientist Paul Ehrlich at a conference exploring the mass extinction of plants and animals. He deduced that 'Scientific analysis points, curiously, towards the need for a quasi-religious transformation of contemporary cultures.'[4]

There is much buried – almost lost – wisdom to help in this transformation from a crucified Earth to one which is the setting for another renaissance and resurrection of the human family, and Nature itself. The cultures and religions of other peoples remind us again and again of the sacredness of the Earth:

> We belong to the ground
> It is our power
> And we must stay close to it
> Or maybe we will get lost.[5]
> (Narritjin Maymuru Yirrkala, an Aborigine)

The mystical tradition, especially as embodied in the works of Hildegard of Bingen and Meister Eckhart, tells repeatedly of the interdependence of everything. For example, Hildegard writes: 'The earth is at the same time Mother. She is Mother of all that is natural, Mother of all that is human. She is the Mother of all for contained in her are the seeds of all.'[6] And again, 'Everything that is in the heaven, on the earth and under the earth is penetrated with connectedness, penetrated with relatedness.'[7]

Unless we recover the sense that the Earth bestows her blessings on humankind, it will not be possible to speak of its holiness. Nevertheless, it is possible to consider corporate holiness. By this I mean that there are groups and communities which can be described as holy. Their life together is perceived as a journey to God. Their horizons are not limited. Everything is offered to God, so that God's just and loving reign may be established more fully.

I think of Mother Teresa, and the community to which she belongs, offering dignity to the dying. I remember the modern martyrs of Central America and Uganda, who offered the most human and transcendent act of all – the sacrifice of their lives – for the sake of justice. There are those who are passionate, radical and inclusive in their love for others. Some are well known such as Dietrich Bonhoeffer, Dorothy Day and Mahatma Gandhi; most are not. Their lives are unnoticed and rarely recorded.

Such people are not 'saints' on some strange 'ego' trip. They and their associates depend on one another; they are intimately involved with and part of churches and communities from which flow support, encouragement and nourishment. And such people are rooted in the history of their time; their holiness emerges as a result of their desire to serve in situations where there is no love. I am not speaking of a privatised holiness but of corporate and collective endeavours to be, as far as it is possible, like Christ.

But 'Christ-likeness' is too one-dimensional and too easy a way of speaking. The people and the churches who may seem to be in some way Christ-like are in fact like us. They are, as Sallie McFague puts it:

> At one level very ordinary human beings battling their own desire for money and comfort, afraid for their families, lonely in prison and frightened of death, discouraged by the slight gains they make against the forces of discrimination, fear, and prejudice that divide people.[8]

Yet they and their communities are the holy people of our day – the saviours of the world.

Nevertheless, even when the ambiguities and contradictions of these communities are understood, is there a sense in which their holiness is beyond us? Are there less exalted manifestations of holiness, grounded in our own history?

There are two. One is the way in which Christian communities respond to strangers when they practise hospitality. The stranger – part of the public 'out there' – is a reminder of our essential unity and interdependence (that word again). We share common space, common resources and common opportunities. The Earth is our home. But our sense of the public has diminished, except as a threat. There are fewer and fewer places where strangers can meet, because intimacy is everything. We have forgotten what strangers can do for us. They draw us out of ourselves and remove the fear we have of one another.

In the Bible, the stranger is the bearer of truth and of promise. To welcome the stranger is not to say, 'Come and join us and be like one of us,' but 'Come and be with us in your distinct and unique way.' Wherever strangers are welcomed, there is a sign of that inclusive and generous love which reflects, however clumsily, the same love which Jesus Christ manifested. (This understanding of the stranger is developed further in Parker J. Palmer's *The Company of Strangers*.[9])

The other mark of corporate holiness is when communities do not engage in deception and cover-ups of one sort or another, but are committed to truth in all its aspects. Churches are masterly at cover-ups. Disagreements and conflicts are invariably stifled because church members have been programmed into thinking that the expression of anger is wrong, and unity and order have to be achieved at any price. The Church as a family is an image which discourages diversity and disagreement. One of the reasons that many experiences of what is called church life are so dismal is that truth does not readily get a look-in. Remarks like 'I don't want to hurt X's feelings' ensure a community life of banality and superficiality.

I have learnt much from women, who have been immobilised in the pews but are now discovering some energy and power among themselves. And one thing they have to teach the Church is how all Christian communities should monitor themselves as to matters of truth. The power of the question is very strong. Sylvia Plath's *The Bell Jar* tells of how we breathe and breathe again our own fetid air, thus subjecting ourselves to more and more delusion.[10] Our capacity for self-delusion, and not facing up to truth because of the pain involved, is yet another way in which our ability to be truly human is severely blunted.

There is no holiness when truth is ignored. Where truth is taken seriously, there is a chance that vitality will emerge. Provided there is a desire to celebrate together and a willingness to handle conflict (however painful, because all human beings have more in common than that which divides them) then it may be said of this or that person, how she has changed, how she has become much more herself. Who would have thought it? Any community where these sorts of comments can be made of all its members shows some marks – maybe bruised and scarred – of the wholeness and holiness of God.

10

WILL OUR CHILDREN HAVE FAITH?

Christianity – Good News for Today?

Most evenings in Leicester Square there are two or three men holding up placards inscribed with biblical texts. They announce the imminent end of the world. Sometimes they quote the words of Jesus (Mark 1:15): 'The time is fulfilled, and the kingdom of God is at hand: repent ye, and believe the gospel.' There follows an invitation to the passerby to repent before it is too late. No one takes any notice of these people or the texts. If I were to join them I would be regarded as yet another religious freak.

However, when Jesus Christ spoke these words, most of his audience welcomed the announcement as the best possible news. They knew precisely what he meant by the Kingdom of God. At last, after all their waiting, suffering and persecution under Roman rule, their hopes for freedom were to be realised in this prophet. And when, after the resurrection, Jesus was proclaimed as Messiah, this news was so welcome that Christian communities grew rapidly in most of the major cities of the Mediterranean. When St Paul preached that the way to God was through faith in Jesus Christ and not in observing all the details of the Mosaic law, his words were greeted with much relief. To sum it up, the Gospel was exciting, inspiring and energising news. It gave hope.

If Christianity is to make any sense today and to be faithful to its founder, it too must convey good news and the hope contained in it. Otherwise, however many appeals may be made to tradition, doctrine and dogma, it will convey nothing. Without hope there is no true religion. Religion may offer comfort, consolation, refuge and sanctuary, but hope is its central characteristic. And as we shall see, the hope offered in the Bible, and in the experience of 2000 years at its best, is not utopian, private, spiritual, romantic, wishful thinking. It is that there should be a more humane future for us all. That tantalising vision is held before us, although the struggle to realise it may seem to be in constant danger of defeat and obliteration.

Therefore, it is essential if Christianity is to speak to us as a message of hope today that it addresses the hopelessness and despair, the apathy, indifference and cynicism which is such a feature of our society. Whenever I take part in conversations about the state of Britain in the 1980s, with all sorts of people – sometimes in a public forum, sometimes more privately – the conversation ends with someone saying, 'Well, we can't do anything about it, can we?'

The list of wrongs is familiar. It includes the deterioration of life in our cities, child beggars, the young homeless, poverty of every sort, racism, violence on the streets, public affluence and public squalor. It might include the sense of disillusionment among civil servants and in the legal profession, the exhaustion of social workers, the humiliation of teachers, the growing power of the police and the erosion of civil liberties. While most of us have improved our 'standard of living' since 1945, many have not. There is a sense that there is something profoundly diseased about society in spite of the material prosperity of those living in the South-East. Yet the sense of hopelessness and impotence – that no one can do anything to improve matters – is the most common reaction both in Britain and internationally.

Hopelessness breeds apathy, and apathy generates indifference. Indifference is the parent of cynicism, the devaluation of public life, the mistrust of the stranger and withdrawal into the sphere of the private and personal where, it is said, true happiness lies. It might be pertinent to ask why, given the fact that we live in a society where freedom is supposedly cherished, we are not in fact free to move out of this negative solidarity of helplessness.

Because so much political and religious discourse does not recognise this deep apathy and indifference, it is deprived of interest and energy. If hope is central to religion, then how does religion address these manifestations of hopelessness and despair? How does one cope with the desperate acts of terrorists, the embrace of conformity of any sort at the expense of truth, and the acceptance of secular and political slogans which discourage questions and criticism?

There are no straightforward, easy answers to these questions. Certainly, as I have said, there is no point in repeating parrot-fashion phrases and doctrines once resonant with meaning but now dying or dead.

Forward from the Bible

A start can be made with the appropriation of the 'memories of our faith'. Walter Brueggemann, in *The Prophetic Imagination*, makes this point:

> The church will not have power to act or believe until it recovers the tradition of faith and permits that tradition to be the primal way out of enculturation. [By 'enculturation' he means the extent to which the Church reflects and endorses dominant opinions and attitudes.] This is not a cry for traditionalism but rather a judgement that the church has no business more pressing than the re-appropriation of its memory in its full power and authenticity.[1]

Recovery, reappropriation and reclamation are key concepts to grasp before Christianity can make sense today, and become a setting for hope. To understand these concepts, we have to consider the way in which the Bible and other ancient, influential texts are used. The Bible is not primarily a collection of books which are to be studied. It is not a static book which provides answers to questions. And it is not a historical curiosity.

The Bible is much more like a tradition which is alive and active among its readers. We listen to what it says, but we also expect to be addressed. In that sense it is like Wagner's Ring Cycle or the corpus of Shakespeare's plays. Producers perceive these operas or plays as in some sense being 'alive'. When these works are reinterpreted for today's audience, there is a crucial interaction between the text and the production – each affects the other.

There is, of course, no definitive, authoritative production which conveys finally, and once and for all, Wagner's or Shakespeare's vision. The producer does the best he can, knowing that in the next generation perspectives he has missed will be discovered by others. In other words, the mystery of great art is not accessible in its entirety all the time to everyone. And if that is true of Wagner or Shakespeare, how much more must it be true of the oddest of holy books. For much of the Bible consists of books written for particular occasions – not to be regarded as definitive statements of truth. These books speak of the way in which men and women have responded to what they have glimpsed of God, particularly through daily events and happenings – through their history.

Recovery of memory depends on becoming an 'insider' – in the very strange world of Jesus or Jeremiah or Solomon or Moses. This means, of course, knowing at least the basic outline of ancient geography and history – not for its own sake or out of some antiquarian interest, but simply to begin to get an inkling of what life was like.

Then begins the process of nurturing a historical imagination – grasping the significance of particular events. This process should not develop an undisciplined fantasy, but help us to discover the images and symbols which people then used to convey profound experiences of suffering, abandonment, loss, as well as those of vitality, energy and newness. As this capacity is developed, so those images and symbols begin to have living possibilities for today. They chime with our present experience and resonance is established. Ancient memories are reappropriated.

I have heard black men and women from South Africa preach sermons about the Exodus and easily, naturally and completely appropriately, describe Mr Botha as the Pharaoh of Egypt. What might seem a naive and over-simplified statement in fact springs from a community downtrodden but struggling, oppressed but hopeful. The simplicity of that image is deceptive. It comes out of a time of testing, refining and 'getting it right' from the depths of their experience.

Some scholars may well scoff at this approach. After all, as we have seen, there is so little we know about Jesus, for example. And if that is true of him, what about Abraham, Moses, the judges, the kings, the prophets and the rest of the cast of the Old Testament? If everything is shrouded in such uncertainty and mystery then it follows logically that we are driven back to our own personal and private journey. We become self-made men and women, helpless before the claims of truth which cannot be denied, having repudiated the historical roots from which we sprang. Such a religion creates an unresolvable anguish that absolutely nothing is certain. Alternatively, it reduces and trivialises religion so that God is individualised, even personalised, and religious faith becomes a panacea for a psychological need. As some Christians say, 'From the day I was introduced to Jesus, my life changed. I get headaches less and less . . .'

But I do not take such a limited view of either the Old Testament or the New Testament. For me, there is enough coherence in the Bible for us to feel our way into the experiences, images and symbols which can convey power, enlarge the imagination and generate God's hope.

When memories are 'appropriated', the collective amnesia which churches sometimes suffer from is dispelled; and the freshness and energy of the tradition is allowed to emerge. And that becomes the first step towards recovering a Judaeo-Christian identity which might free itself from 'enculturation'. This horrible word is best explained as 'saturation' – saturation of the churches by capitalism which, as Jeremy Seabrook says:

lives through us, and inhabits us with such oppressive density that it fills our eyes and ears, all our senses, our imaginations and our minds, with the images, the fantasies, as well as the common sense, indeed, the logic of its own necessities.[2]

The recovery of our tradition means making connections between then and now, between what was going on then and what is going on now. Looking back does not mean being identified with the Fundamentalism of Conservative Evangelicals whose slogans and texts point their hearers to the possibilities and rewards of life hereafter, while ignoring the relevance of the prophetic word for today. Looking back to the unusual ancestry of Christianity often does not appeal to liberals who may well consider themselves too sophisticated to be lumbered with such a particular history.

What happens when amnesia is dispelled, and the Bible is allowed to breathe? First, its oddness immediately becomes apparent, for the Bible is discovered as a literature of hope. Our cultural tradition does not have much to say about hope: we are illiterate about its meaning. Instead we have come to accept that everything is understood through the process of discovery, dissection and experiment. We seek to understand in order to control so that order may be established.

Hope does not fit easily into this scenario of 'knowing' and 'order', for hope expresses a conviction that there is an overriding purpose to the whole of history, which will oddly but definitely prevail. The stories about Abraham, Isaac and Jacob in Genesis are about the open-ended promises that God makes: promises of heirs, a new land and a community which is blessed among nations. The prophetic voices of the eighth century state that God has no commitment to the world as it is, but that a new order will be established in God's own time.

Such is the vision of Micah 4:1-5 when swords are beaten into ploughshares, and spears into pruning hooks. Another is that of Ezekiel 34:25 and 27 which promises a new world of prosperity in which Creation will be restored, and oppression brought to an end:

> And I will make with them a covenant of peace, and will cause the evil beasts to cease out of the land: and they shall dwell safely . . . And the tree of the field shall yield her fruit, and the earth shall yield her increase, and they shall be safe in their land.

Perhaps the most generous, most liberated vision of them all is found in Isaiah 65:17–25:

> For, behold, I create new heavens and a new earth: and the former shall not be remembered, nor come into mind. But be ye glad and rejoice for ever in that which I create: for, behold, I create Jerusalem a rejoicing, and her people a joy. And I will rejoice in Jerusalem, and joy in my people: and the voice of weeping shall be no more heard in her, nor the voice of crying. There shall be no more thence an infant of days, nor an old man that hath not filled his days: for the child shall die an hundred years old; but the sinner being an hundred years old shall be accursed. And they shall build houses, and inhabit them; and they shall plant vineyards, and eat the fruit of them. They shall not build, and another inhabit; they shall not plant, and another eat: for as the days of a tree are the days of my people, and mine elect shall long enjoy the work of their hands. They shall not labour in vain, nor bring forth trouble; for they are the seed of the blessed of the Lord, and their offspring with them. And it shall come to pass, that before they call, I will answer; and while they are yet speaking, I will hear. The wolf and the lamb shall feed together, and the lion shall eat straw like the bullock: and dust shall be the serpent's meat. They shall not hurt nor destroy in all my holy mountain, saith the Lord.

The persecution of the Jewish people before the Christian era led to the formulation of extravagant visions and dreams of restoration, justice, order and peace. And, as we have seen, the early days of Christianity were filled with excitement and anticipation. Today both Jews and Christians wait for a God who will 'mend the world', which surely means that all our present arrangements – political systems, economic systems and religious institutions – should be provisional, for only God is absolute.

Religious hope should not be divorced from history, from what has happened and is happening in the world. The promise of a new order appears on the expanding horizon, to which our steps are leading. Nevertheless, this kind of hope is not easy to come by. It is not cheap grace. Before that hope can be experienced in all its amazing and astonishing vitality, much else has to happen.

Jeremiah and Jesus

The Old Testament prophets are the key to regaining vitality. Prophets are normally regarded as fierce and stern. They appear briefly, breathing hell fire and preaching gloom and doom; then they disappear, ranting and whacking people on the head!

But this is a misinterpretation. The prophets are poets first and foremost. They speak of endings and beginnings. Through their images, and poetry, they say that the known world of public institutions, temple and monarchy, is coming to an end. They do not say when; they do not provide a timetable. But they interpret events, the history of their day, through the eyes of God. Jeremiah is the best example of such a prophet. He lived at a crucial point in Israel's history – some 2600 years ago. In 587 BC the Temple in Jerusalem was destroyed and King David's dynasty, which had ruled for nearly 500 years, came to an end. Every recognisable form of public life ceased.

Politically, the end of Judah was a result of the rapid expansion of the Babylonian Empire. But Jeremiah perceived this ending of a nation as a judgement of God. His characteristic poems neither scold nor reprimand. In Jeremiah 4:19-20, he expresses his grief that the beloved kingdom of Judah is no more; and no one has even noticed:

> My bowels, my bowels! I am pained at my very heart; my heart maketh a noise in me; I cannot hold my peace, because thou hast heard, O my soul, the sound of the trumpet, the alarm of war. Destruction upon destruction is cried; for the whole land is spoiled: suddenly are my tents spoiled, and my curtains in a moment.

The destruction of his country reaches his bedroom door; his heart breaks. The poet is terrified.

In common with all the prophets, Jeremiah criticises the rich for their unjust treatment of the poor. He attacks the false prophets, and those who say 'Peace, peace' when there is no peace. He speaks of a cancer alive in the state. Time and again he reminds his listeners how helpless they are, because they have cut themselves off from their roots, and from their identity.

Jeremiah's grief expresses the pain God feels for his people; the prophet's grief also seems to criticise Judah, and psychologically to upset and dismantle the political, social and economic reality of the time. And it is this dismantling which gives way to energising hope for the future. Jeremiah's poetry is more about the imagination than the implementation of fresh policies. Time and again the threats, grief and hopelessness give way to a note of promise. God will never desert his people. In Jeremiah 30:12 and 13, the prophet draws on metaphors of illness and injury to describe the condition of Judah: 'For thus saith the Lord, Thy bruise is incurable, and thy wound grievous. There is none to plead thy cause, that thou mayest be bound up; thou hast no healing medicines.' In verse 14, Judah is now deserted, and quite alone: 'All thy lovers have forgotten thee; they seek thee not, for I have wounded thee with the chastisement of a cruel one, for the multitude of thine iniquity; because thy sins were increased.' Judah is regarded as unreliable because of her self-interest and self-aggrandisement, and she has been deserted by her former allies – her 'lovers'. Once upon a time Judah had been treated as a partner in the covenant which God had made with her people, but now God sees Judah as the enemy (verse 17): 'Why criest thou for thine affliction? thy sorrow is incurable for the multitude of thine iniquity: because thy sins were increased, I have done these things unto thee.' The rejection is complete. There is no more to say.

Then, in verses 16 and 17, God's assurance is suddenly given. The word 'Therefore' is the key:

Therefore all they that devour thee shall be devoured; and all thine adversaries, every one of them, shall go into captivity; and they that spoil thee shall be a spoil, and all that prey upon thee will I give for a prey. For I will restore health unto thee, and I will heal thee of thy wounds, saith the Lord; because they called thee an Outcast, saying, This is Zion, whom no man seeketh after.

It is easy to miss the significance of this movement from punishment and threat to assurance and restoration. God is not always with his people. There was a break – an abyss – between them; the covenant had been broken. But God, through Jeremiah's lamentation, expressed his grief, his sorrow and his pain that his chosen people had been mocked ('because they called thee an Outcast'). And from this public expression of suffering, hope emerges.

Jeremiah's warnings about endings were not heeded. The kings were naturally satisfied with the status quo; they said, 'for what we have received may we be always thankful – forever and forever'. The powerful desire no change. Hence the continual arguments over the centuries in the Old Testament between the prophets and the monarchs. The magicians, the interpreters of dreams, and the wise men who served the kings in their courts – perhaps the consultants and senior civil servants in our day – were equally reluctant to hear the prophetic word. They were employed by the government. The managers of the royal palaces and the hired intellectuals liked everything to carry on as normal. (Some agreement could surely be made with Babylon!)

Hope is discovered and given, in both the Old Testament and the Gospels, when suffering is out in the open. When grief is expressed and speech takes over from silence, when endings are not only noted but embraced, then hope emerges. And as Walter Brueggemann says:

the primal act of hope in the Bible is the Exodus . . . Out of it comes a certitude that God will sooner or later bring justice and freedom into the world, even for slaves, even against empires. That certitude, however, was not arrived at easily. It arose from the oppressed people around Moses who made bricks for the Egyptian Empire. In the face of Pharaoh they groaned; they cried out; they protested; they raged. They expressed their common misery in public speech, which must have been an incredibly dangerous thing to do. Such common misery brought to public speech is a force in history that neither the tyrannical Pharaoh nor the great God above can ignore. It is written in this story of hope in that 'God heard their groaning, and God remembered his covenant . . . And God saw the people of Israel, and God knew their condition.'[3]

I have made this brief excursion into a minute slice of our history partly because the Jewish Bible (the Old Testament) is so often ignored, and partly to illustrate ways in which these ancient texts and stories are relevant today and may at times provide resonance for us.

The prophetic tradition is focused in Jesus. He too announces endings. He engages in a radical critique of every aspect of human life. The authentic memories of the early Church are about how Jesus, this holy man, rabbi and prophet, showed decisive solidarity with people on the margins of society. Soon he was regarded as a troublemaker and a threat. After all, Jesus forgave sin (something which only God could do), he healed on the Sabbath, he ate with the riff-raff of Palestine and confronted the authorities who ran the Temple. Sooner or later he had to be removed.

The interpretation of the crucifixion by the Gospel writers reveals how devastating Jesus's critique had been. The words from the Cross, preserved in different traditions, are decisive in their criticisms, yet hint at something else – possibilities is too strong a word. Mark 15:15 tells us that Pilate, 'willing to content the people, released Barabbas unto them, and delivered Jesus, when he had scourged him, to be crucified'.

When Jesus forgives his enemies as he is dying, he is saying that the world has been on trial. And it has gone insane, however much life may appear to be normal and controlled. In Mark 15:34 he cries out 'Eloi, Eloi, lama sabachthani?', which means 'My God, my God, why hast thou forsaken me?' And in this cry of despair and abandonment, he asserts that the whole framework of belief and all the received ways of understanding experience have been shattered.

Luke 23:46 recounts his last words: 'Father, into thy hands I commend my spirit.' And with these words, he dies. When Jesus gives in, gives up and hands over, he challenges the system which believes in control and order at any cost. In Luke 23:43 he says, 'Verily I say unto thee, today shalt thou be with me in paradise.' And when he welcomes the criminal into Paradise, it is the marginalised person who is welcomed. In other words, the death of Jesus reflects the chaos, turbulence and darkness of a world which he declared, as the prophets before him, was ending.

But that is not all. Jesus's ministry was good news for the poor. If he was regarded as a threat by those who held religious and political power, he was certainly not regarded as such by those who had experienced his compassion. They knew what it was to have been healed and restored; they experienced the lifting of their humiliation and the discovery of their dignity as daughters and sons of God – a God who was truly with them and for them.

Above all else, the resurrection is a sign of the grace and power of God. While there will always be discussions about what happened, and how it happened, for me the resurrection only begins to make sense in the context of all the amazing alternative futures which the prophets had suggested – always out of their own grief and their own suffering. Walter Brueggemann puts it like this:

> Without detracting from the historical singularity of the resurrection, we can also affirm that it is of a piece with the earlier appearances of an alternative future by the prophetic word. The resurrection of Jesus made possible a future for the disinherited. In the same way, the alternative community of Moses was given a new future by the God who brought freedom for slaves by his powerful word, which both dismantled and created a future and which engaged in radical energising and radical criticising.[4]

If Christianity is a religion of hope, then we have to wake up to God in the pressures and conflicts in our history. If there is no sense at all of God in what is happening to each of us, in our communities, in the world, then not only does religion cease to offer any hope, it becomes a little more than a toy or a drug. If there is to be a lively, hopeful faith in God which our children and their children will live by, nothing is more urgent than waking up to the ways in which God is real and present for us today. There are three areas where such an exploration is fruitful.

From Brokenness to Hope

Jeremiah and Jesus (and many before and since) have spoken of endings. Today, we need to hear the voices of those who speak with apprehension of the ending of the world as we know it (not necessarily in apocalyptic terms, with times and dates and lurid fantasies of how it will happen). Lesslie Newbigin, in *The Other Side of 1984*, puts it like this:

> Science and technology are seen more as threats than as ground for hope. The rise of the 'green' movements as significant political forces is the most obvious sign of this shift in perspective. Science, even in its most benign form as medical science, is now regarded with a scepticism unthinkable fifty years ago. Nearly all the great killing diseases have been mastered in principle, yet the burden on health services in all the western nations is outstripping resources. And the most rapidly growing illnesses are – significantly – those which can be classified broadly as mental, illnesses which are related to the collapse of meaning. Politicians, when out of office, continue to claim that they have solutions for our problems, but their claims are viewed with growing scepticism. The loss of confidence in the future is expressed eloquently in the mindless folly of the petty vandalism of those who can only express their rage by smashing up the symbols of meaningless affluence, and the equally mindless madness of the nuclear arms race between the superpowers. The mushroom clouds which rose into the sky above the blasted ruins of Hiroshima and Nagasaki have, ever since that day in 1945, hung in menace over the consciousness of modern men and women, posing with fearful poignancy the question: 'Is there a future for civilisation as we know it?'[5]

There is a need to voice these questions publicly, and to express the anxiety and confusion as well as suffering and grief of our own day. And there is the grief of those who suffer too much to speak for themselves, as well as those whose voices reach us only fitfully and occasionally. The grief is not just in humankind. Matthew Fox writes in *The Coming of the Cosmic Christ*:

> Is Mother Earth herself not the ultimate anawim [literally: 'little one'], the most neglected of the suffering, voiceless ones today? And along with her, the soil, forests, species, birds and waters are not being heard where legislators gather, where judges preside and where believers gather for worship.[6]

The denial of suffering has had a brutalising and numbing effect on the human spirit. The cover-up in which we all take part may well have its origin in our failure to address our collective guilt about the Holocaust, Hiroshima and Nagasaki. Although these events occurred in the past they haunt us because of the immensity of suffering that was caused and our collusion in it. No reparation has yet been offered. Perhaps if it had been offered, compassion of the sort I have described would now be becoming a reality instead of a nice sentiment.

If we do nothing about those who starve or suffer injustice or die through neglect, it is not because we do not know what to do, it is because the will to do anything has evaporated. And that is because the guilt and the pain have not been acknowledged. There has to be lamentation before celebration and it is indicative of the strength of our individual and corporate denial that we no longer know how to wail, how to lament. We have no language, no tools to do this. Meanwhile the effects of this cover-up are all around: apathy, restlessness and insane outbreak of violence.

This is why the prophets and Jesus Christ are essential in helping us to form a new alternative consciousness. Hope springs from the embracing of dyings and endings. Vitality and energy are forged out of the interface of death and resurrection. Mourning – public and private – is the precondition of hope. The hope of God comes from nowhere else, and the words of Jesus, in Matthew 5:4, say it all: 'Blessed are they that mourn, for they shall be comforted.'

Celebration

I have not written about the Church in this book. There are many paths to explore before reaching the labyrinths of institutional religion. And making sense of religion is rather like clearing the ground before any detailed attention can be given to the Church. With all its confusion and frailty, it is the framework in which some of the insights and explanations of this book are contained.

Nevertheless, one aspect of the Church needs to be considered – the activity which distinguishes it from all other voluntary organisations – that is, its worship. For good or ill, worship (what is said, sung or done) helps to define the attitudes and perspectives not only of individuals but also of the worshipping community. 'Going to church' is the one agreed and obvious activity which identifies a person as a Christian.

It is therefore astonishing that the experience of worship is so boring; and that young people are so conspicuous by their absence (except in Conservative Evangelical churches). In *For God's Sake*[7] I examined why this was so. Here, I want to suggest what can be done to redeem worship so that it bears the character of celebration.

Above all else, worship needs to be set in the context of a God within the cosmos and Creation. Worship has the power to make people attentive and mindful of their inheritance of a 20-billion-year history. And it can reawaken their gratitude and responsibility for this inheritance. The sense of being at home in the universe is a profound and healing experience; it is the grace and interdependence without which there is no acknowledgement of life. Connections are established – within oneself, between all humankind and with Creation. The universe is the primary sacrament in all its teeming mystery and vastness, which express the mystery and beauty of God, and for which Creation can be thankful.

But such gratitude and the mindfulness which creates it are missing. It is that 'something more' which is missed. And this leads to the boring and trivial nature of so much worship. Inevitably it has become almost entirely anthropocentric. The priest faces the people. His personality and the way he leads the worship dictate whether or not it is boring. The prayers often do little more than fill God in with the news: anger, despair, dismay, lamentation or yearning are usually absent. The drive to make the Church a community, expressed in the kiss of peace – the mutual greeting of all, may be right for some people but can be quite disabling for those who do not want or need that enforced close experience. Sometimes church services of almost any denomination have the feeling of meetings which have gone a bit askew. The churches will be slowly abandoned unless the ritual celebrates the blessing of Creation.

To take Creation seriously means treating our bodies seriously – for which we can all take responsibility. Each of us is a body (and more) but worship ignores the body. Kneeling has almost disappeared. The Anglican crouch has taken its place – hands on the pew or the shelf of the pew, with the bottom resting on the seat, and the knees on a hassock. In this position, the body is twisted and discomfort soon sets in.

Furthermore, the new service books (in use in most churches today) entail the collecting of a small library. The hands are rarely free except to hold one of the books, where the words of the prayers are found. No wonder that I have heard young people describe worship as being back at school. The way we stand or sit or move in worship is as important as what is heard or sung.

Given the Church's traditional fears about the body, it is not surprising that all the experiences of touching, of movement and of dance are avoided. But it can be done. For some years, I was involved in pioneering the use of dance and movement in celebrations. It took time for the dancers to develop a vocabulary which was understood by those who were not dancing. Alongside parts of the celebrations which were danced, circle dancing and many forms of processions took place. Everyone took part if they wished to. No one was excluded because they were not the right shape. And in the context of a celebration where attention was given to what was seen, sung, smelt, heard and touched, the dance – both of the group and of the entire community, of children and adults – was not exceptional. It became part of the celebration.

Celebration needs to be experienced as something joyful. I do not mean the grim cheerfulness and intense smiling of some churches, but joy which reflects the delight and pleasure in Creation, and in one another. Music is the key to the expression of this joy. I believe there is a movement away from singing the hymns found in our established hymn books to music which is direct, simple, accessible and expressive.

Joy is only one aspect of celebration – the other is a recognition of the darkness and the suffering. Nowhere in our Prayer Book is there a space for lamentation. Suffering needs to be expressed; pain has to come out. We have to discover how to mourn, how to wail, how to lament, and this can be learnt from those communities which have experienced slavery, and from women, who have been immobilised and exiled. It will involve learning how to be silent, and how to welcome the darkness in worship. It is possible and desirable to pray and celebrate together in darkness or semi-darkness as well as in the light. The darkness allows for silence, for grief and for growth.

Who is to arrange all these celebrations? There is no one other than ourselves to do so; an ecclesiastical, liturgical communion will not be of much use. It means a deliberate attempt to place ourselves deeply within our Christian tradition so that we will then feel at home anywhere.

But what our celebrations are crying out for are the resources of our imaginations: of the poet, composer, musician, artist, sculptor, film-maker, and choreographer. Celebrations need all creative artists, and all the creativity within each one of us. The artist helps us bring to birth images and sounds, both very ancient and new, which foster a consciousness of an alternative and human future. The artist stimulates, corrects and suggests, but we need to find our own meanings. There will be no celebration without the artist, whose banishment from the churches is as serious a sin as the exclusion of the poor.

The Transcendence of God

When God is co-opted by the Church, then true religion dies. Religion becomes narrow, predictable and domesticated. It is of no interest, and cannot draw on the passion of anyone except those for whom God has been tamed. The worst type of co-option in the Bible is that of Solomon and the Temple.

Solomon created a prosperous Empire – for some. He had the army under his thumb; he built up an elaborate bureaucracy, and a substantial harem so that his monarchy would be self-generating. He had a bevy of teachers of wisdom. But his social policy was oppressive; it depended on enforced slave labour. Criticism of any sort was not tolerated. And the oppression of some and the affluence of most was supported by religion, by the Temple. The Temple was also under the control of the King. God had been taken captive.

God was accessible, and provided the necessary respectability for the monarchy. God's accessibility creates a constant tension for the minister of religion. When asked to say grace at a public function, he is expected to perform, because he has ready access to God by virtue of his office. But the minister will also know something about God's freedom. God cannot be co-opted into politics or religion. If God is a God of hope then all present arrangements are provisional; there is no way in which God can be assimilated.

God's transcendence is manifested whenever we are called out beyond ourselves to create something of beauty, to ask for forgiveness for injustice, or to serve those in any sort of need. Salvation and healing cannot be present realities – they are never ever completed – in this life.

If we are prepared to learn how to weep, to celebrate in the setting of God's Creation, and to acknowledge the holiness of a God who can never be co-opted, then that hope which is the heart of religion will shine, and our children may have faith.

NOTES AND
FURTHER READING

Chapter 1   Making Sense

1   David E. Jenkins, *God, Politics and the Future*, SCM Press Ltd, London, 1988, p. ix

2   Ruben Alves, *What is Religion?*, Orbis Books, London, 1984, p. 90

3   Simone Weil, *Waiting for God*, Harper & Row, New York, 1973, p. 32

4   Sallie McFague, *Models of God*, SCM Press Ltd, London, 1987, p. 192. Sallie McFague's extensive writings on Metaphorical Theology have been an important influence in writing this book – particularly in this chapter, Chapter 3 and Chapter 4.

5   A. H. Hodges, *God Beyond Knowledge,* Macmillan Ltd, London, 1979, p. 9. Quoted in David E. Jenkins, *God, Miracle and the Church of England*, SCM Press Ltd, London, 1987, p. 10.

6   Kenneth Leech, *True God*, Sheldon Press, London, 1985, p. 25

7   Monica Furlong, *Travelling In*, Hodder and Stoughton, London, 1971, p. 14

8   Gerard W. Hughes, *In Search of a Way*, Darton, Longman & Todd, London, 1986, p. 50. Gerard Hughes is also the author of *God of Surprises* (Darton, Longman & Todd). Both books are classics of contemporary spirituality.

9   John Bowden, *Jesus: The Unanswered Questions*, SCM Press Ltd, London, 1988, p. 185. John Bowden brings together many of the

unanswered questions about Jesus in a most accessible way. As
Editor and Managing Director of SCM Press, he has probably read
almost everything there is to read about Jesus!

10   Graham Greene, *The Honorary Consul*, Simon & Schuster, New
York, 1973, p. 66
11   Albert Nolan, *God in South Africa: The Challenge of the Gospel*,
Catholic Institute for International Relations, London, 1988, p. 15

Chapter 2   Idolatory and Imagination

1   Jeremy Seabrook and Trevor Blackwell, *The Politics of Hope*, Faber & Faber, London, 1988, p. 63

2   Jeremy Seabrook, *What Went Wrong?*, Gollancz, London, 1978. Quoted in Seabrook and Blackwell, op. cit., p. 63

3   Bob Goudzwarrd, *Idols of our Time*, Inter Varsity Press, Illinois, 1984, p. 21

4   Alasdair MacIntyre, 'A Society without a Metaphysics', *The Listener*, 30 September, 1956. Quoted in Leech, op. cit., p. 20

5   John F. Kamanough, 'Spirituality and Culture – Capitalist Culture and Christian Faith', *The Way*, July 1985, No. 3

6   Dennis Nineham in J. Hick (ed.) *The Myth of God Incarnate*, SCM Press Ltd, London, 1977, pp. 201–2

7   Ruben Alves, op. cit., p. 18

Chapter 3 Creation as the Body of God

1   Ian G. Barbour, *Myths, Models and Paradigms: A Comparative Study in Science and Religion*, Harper & Row, New York, 1974, p. 156. Quoted in McFague, op. cit., p. 63

2   David E. Jenkins, *God, Miracle and the Church of England*, SCM Press Ltd, London, 1987, p. 4

3   Thomas Berry, 'Our Children: Their Future', in *The Little Magazine*, Bear & Co., Vol. 1, No. 10, p. 8

4   Julian of Norwich, *Revelations of Divine Love*, Little Gidding Books, Chapter 5

5   Julian of Norwich, op. cit. This section is often edited out in modern versions of the work, but is present in critical editions. It is quoted in Matthew Fox, *Original Blessing*, Bear & Co Inc., Santa Fe, p. 64

6   Thomas Traherne, *Centuries of Meditations*, edited and published by Bertrand Dobell, London, 1950. Quoted in *The English Spirit*, Darton, Longman & Todd, London, 1987, p. 20.

7   William Blake, *Complete Writings*, ed. by Sir Geoffrey Keynes, Oxford University Press, Oxford, 1969

8   Gerard Manley Hopkins, 'God's Grandeur' in *Poems and Prose of Gerard Manley Hopkins*, Penguin Books, London, 1953

9   Thomas Berry, op. cit.

10   Sallie McFague, op. cit., pp. 8–9

11   Donald Nicholl, *Holiness*, Darton, Longman & Todd, London, 1987, p. 20. Published and copyright 1981 by Darton, Longman & Todd and is used by permission of the publishers.

Chapter 4   God as Mother

1   Edward Schillebeeckx, *Christ*, SCM Press Ltd, London, 1980. Quoted in Bowden, op. cit., p. 190

2   Dorothy Sölle, *Choosing Life*, SCM Press Ltd, London, 1981, p. 68

3   Kenneth Leech, op. cit., p. 350

4   E. O. James, *The Cult of the Mother Goddess*, Barnes & Noble, New York, 1959

5   Rosemary Radford Reuther, *Womanguides: Readings toward a Feminist Theology*, Beacon Press, Boston, 1985, p. 105

6   Hans Urs von Balthasar, *Elucidations*, SPCK, London, 1974, p. 72. Quoted in Leech, op. cit., p. 369

Chapter 5   Jesus Christ – Living with Questions

1 Bertolt Brecht, *Life of Galileo*, in *Plays: Three*, trans. by John Willett, Methuen, London, 1987

2 Ibid., p. 82

3 John Bowden, op. cit., p. 24

4 David Jenkins, quoted in Ted Harrison, *The Durham Phenomenon*, Darton, Longman & Todd, London, 1985, p. 49

5 Bernard Ramm, *The Christian View of Science and Scripture*, quoted in James Barr, *Fundamentalism*, SCM Press Ltd, London, 1981, p. 94

6 Ibid., p. 68

7 *Collected Poems of Louis MacNeice*, Faber & Faber, London, 1966

8 Robert L. Wilken, *The Myth of Christian Beginnings*, SCM Press Ltd, London, 1979, p. 185

9 Dennis Nineham, 'The Strangeness of the New Testament World', *Theology*, 1985

10 James H. Cone, *God of the Oppressed*, Seabury Press, London, 1975. Quoted in Bowden, op. cit., p. 102

11 Samuel Rayan, 'Where do we go from here?', *Concilium*, No. 199

Chapter 6 Guilt, Sin, Salvation and Atonement

1 Harry Williams, 'Theology and Self Awareness', in A. R. Vidler (ed.), *Soundings*, Cambridge University Press, Cambridge, 1962, p. 79

2 Jacques Pohier, *God in Fragments*, SCM Press Ltd, London, 1985, pp. 202–54. The whole of this chapter is remarkable for the author's analysis of the place of guilt in Christianity.

3 Ibid.

4 Sallie McFague, op. cit., p. 150

5 Ibid., p. 151

6 Dietrich Bonhoeffer, *Letters and Papers from Prison*, SCM Press Ltd, London, 1967, p. 172

Chapter 7   Evil and Suffering

1   Hannah Arendt, *Eichmann in Jerusalem: A Report on the Banality of Evil*, Viking Press, New York, 1964

2   Albert Nolan, op. cit., p. 86

3   William Shakespeare, *Macbeth*, Collins, London, 1951, Act II, Scene IV

4   Subniv Babuta and Jean-Claude Bragard, *Evil*, Weidenfeld & Nicolson, London, 1988, p. 40

5   W. Somerset Maugham, *The Summing Up*, Pan Books, London, 1976

6   David Hume, *Dialogues concerning Natural Religion*, Harper & Row, New York, 1948, p. 66

7   Kenneth Surin, *Theology and the Problem of Evil*, Basil Blackwell, Oxford, 1986, p. 147

8   Irving Greenberg, *Cloud of Smoke, Pillar of Fire: Judaism, Christianity and Modernity after the Holocaust.* Quoted in Surin, op. cit.

9   Elie Wiesel, *The Gates of the Forest*, trans. by Frances Frenaye, Holt, Reinhart & Winston, New York, 1966, p. 197

10   John Hick, *Evil and the God of Love*, Macmillan & Co, London, 1985, p. 171

11   Albert Nolan, op. cit., p. 57

12   W. H. Vanstone, *Love's Endeavour, Love's Expense*, Darton, Longman & Todd, London, 1977. This is the best exposition of the phenomenology of love that I know.

13   Dorothy Sölle, 'God's Pain and Our Pain: How theology had to change after Auschwitz'. A paper presented to the International Scholars Conference, 'Remembering for the Future', held at Oxford, 10–13 July 1988. Pergamon Press, Oxford, 1988, p. 461

Chapter 8   Compassion

1   Thomas Merton, 'Marxism and Monastic Perspectives', quoted in John Moffitt (ed.), *A New Charter for Monasticism*, University of Notre Dame Press, Indiana, 1970, p. 80

2   Lewis Thomas, 'The Lives of a Cell' in *The Wonderful Mistake*, Oxford University Press, Oxford, 1988

3   Jon Wynne-Tyson (ed.), *The Extended Circle*, Centaur Press, Arundel, Sussex, 1985, p. 139

4   Ibid., p. 122

5   Gregory of Nyssa, quoted in Matthew Fox, *A Spirituality named Compassion*, Harper & Row, New York, 1979

6   For the analysis of Jacob's ladder and Sarah's circle I am greatly indebted to Matthew Fox, op. cit.

7   Abraham Herschel, 'Last words: An Interview by Carl Stern', in *Intellectual Digest*, June 1973, p. 78

Chapter 9   Together?

1   Donald Nicholl, op. cit., p. 27

2   Wendell Berry, 'The Body and the Earth'

3   Rainer Rilke, quoted in Matthew Fox, *Original Blessing*, Bear & Co, Santa Fe, p. 152

4   Matthew Fox, *The Coming of the Cosmic Christ*, Harper & Row, New York, 1988, p. 2. This book develops a Green theology and a theology of liberation for the western world.

5   Quoted in Fox, *The Coming of the Cosmic Christ*, p. 11

6   *Illuminations of Hildegard of Bingen*, with a commentary by Matthew Fox, Bear & Co, 1985, Santa Fe, p. 11

7   Ibid., p. 19

8   Sallie McFague, op. cit., pp. 151–2

9   Parker J. Palmer, *The Company of Strangers*, Crossroad Publishing Co, New York, 1983. Although written for American readers, this book is relevant for our own society; it urges a renewal of citizenship and public life.

10 Sylvia Plath, *The Bell Jar*, Faber & Faber, London, 1966

Chapter 10 Will Our Children Have Faith?

1 Walter Brueggemann, *The Prophetic Imagination*, Fortress Press, Philadelphia, 1978, p. 12

2 Blackwell and Seabrook, op. cit.

3 Walter Brueggemann, *Hope within History*, John Knox Press, Atlanta, 1987, p. 87

4 Walter Brueggemann, *The Prophetic Imagination*, p. 107

5 Lesslie Newbigin, *The Other Side of 1984*, World Council of Churches, 1983, p. 2

6 Matthew Fox, *The Coming of the Cosmic Christ*, p. 17

7 Donald Reeves, *For God's Sake*, Collins, London, 1988

Quotations from the Bible have been taken from the Authorised Version.